Revelation

Worthy Is the Lamb

To Him who sits on the throne and to the Lamb
be praise and honor and glory and power for ever and ever!

Revelation 5:13

Prepared by Dale E. Griffin, Julene Dumit,
and Rodney L. Rathmann

Contributions by Robert C. Baker

CONCORDIA PUBLISHING HOUSE · SAINT LOUIS

Copyright © 1994, 2005 Concordia Publishing House
3558 S. Jefferson Ave., St. Louis, MO 63118-3968
1-800-325-3040 · www.cph.org

Prepared by Dale E. Griffin, Julene Dumit, and Rodney L. Rathmann

Edited by Robert C. Baker

Unless otherwise indicated, Scripture quotations are from the HOLY BIBLE, NEW INTERNATIONAL VERSION®. NIV®. Copyright © 1973, 1978, 1984 by International Bible Society. Used by permission of Zondervan Publishing House. All rights reserved.

The Scripture quotation marked NET is taken from the *HOLY BIBLE: New Testament—New Evangelical Translation.* Copyright © 1992 God's Word To The Nations Bible Society. Used by permission.

The quote by W. Hendriksen is from *More Than Conquerors,* copyright © 1979 Baker Publishing Group. Used by permission.

Material from *Revelation: The Distant Triumph Song* by Siegbert W. Becker copyright © 1985 Northwestern Publishing House, Milwaukee, WI. Used by permission.

Excursus on Resurrection of the Body is taken from *The End Times: A Study on Eschatology and Millennialism* (St. Louis: Commission on Theology and Church Relations of The Lutheran Church—Missouri Synod, September, 1989) pp. 27–29. Used by permission.

Excursus on The Lamb of God from *Revelation* (part of *The Concordia Commentary Series*) by Louis A. Brighton. Copyright © 1999 Concordia Publishing House. Used by permission.

This publication may be available in □raille, in large print, or on cassette tape for the visually impaired. Please allow 8 to 12 weeks for delivery. Write to the Library for the Blind, 7550 Watson Rd., St. Louis, MO 63119-4409; call toll-free 1-888-215-2455; or visit the Web site: www.blindmission.org.

Manufactured in the United States of America

1 2 3 4 5 6 7 8 9 10   15 14 13 12 11 10 09 08 07 06 05

Contents

History	Date (A.D.)	John
Crucifixion, resurrection, and ascension of Christ	30	John accepts earthly care of Jesus' mother, Mary
Descent of the Holy Spirit in Jerusalem	30	
Caligula Roman Emperor	37–41	
Claudius Roman Emperor	41–54	
Jerusalem Council	49/50	
	50–70	Early dates of John's Gospel
Nero Roman Emperor	54–68	
Paul imprisoned in Rome	59–61/62	
	ca. 66	John begins ministry in Ephesus
Peter crucified upside down in Rome	67	
Paul beheaded in Rome	67/68	
Jerusalem captured and Temple destroyed	70	
Domitian Roman Emperor	81–96	
	85 and later	Traditional dates of John's Gospel and three epistles
	90–95	John exiled on Patmos
	95	Traditional date of John's Revelation
	ca. 100	John dies in Ephesus

An Outline of Revelation

Introduction

*"Salvation belongs to our God, who sits upon the throne,
and to the Lamb."*

Revelation 7:10

If sales of religious books dealing with the end times reliably indicate the nation's spiritual appetite, one could say there is a deep hunger in the land. Since the 1970's readers have devoured such titles as *Late Great Planet Earth* by Hal Lindsey, and more recently the *Left Behind* book series by Tim LaHaye and Jerry Jenkins (to date over 60 million copies sold). Is there a reason for such a craving of end times Christian literature?

A core teaching in many popular end times materials, including the *Left Behind* series, is the so-called rapture. According to this theory Christ will secretly take to heaven living believers and young infants and children prior to His second coming. There are widely divergent views as to the origin of this teaching:

- Welsh-born Baptist, Morgan Edwards, alludes to a secret "rapture" in book he published in 1788. The title page of his work quotes Acts 17:19–20: "May we know what this new teaching is that you are presenting? You are bringing some strange ideas to our ears, and we want to know what they mean";
- Chilean Jesuit Manual (or Emmanuel) Lacunza published a book on the rapture in 1812. Lacunza's writings, under Hebrew pen name Ben Ezra, were eventually banned by the Roman Catholic Church due to their false teaching;
- Scotsman Edward Irving published an English translation of Lacunza's work in 1827. Irving (whose followers are sometimes called Irvingites) promoted Pentecostal phenomena, and was eventually defrocked by the Church of Scotland for his anti-Trinitarian views;
- Englishman John Nelson Darby discovered the "rapture" in 1827 after realizing that the church is not Israel (some

speculate Darby read Irving's translation of Lacunza). Darby systematized dispensationalist theology, which emphasizes a literal 1,000-year reign of Christ upon earth;

- Scottish teenager Margaret MacDonald received rapture teaching through an ecstatic religious experience in 1830 (some surmise Darby may have received the teaching from MacDonald). MacDonald's family was involved in Pentecostal phenomena including regularly speaking in "tongues."

No matter its actual provenance, John Nelson Darby preached about the rapture (and dispensationalism) in a series of engagements from 1859 to 1874 in the United States and Canada. The teaching received further promotion in Great Britain and the United States through the *Scofield Reference Bible*, first published by C. I. Scofield in 1909. Scofield's notes and annotations have provided source material for Lindsey, LaHaye and Jenkins, and others. Interestingly, the secret rapture, along with dispensationalism, has not been widely received by Christians outside of the United States and Canada.

Perhaps popular end times literature offers to satisfy a gnawing desire for a manifestation of Christ's power and presence in our lives. Maybe complicated Bible mysteries—solved by experts offering tailor-made explanations—offer a soothing diversion from our increasingly complicated existence. Perchance we pine for a quick deliverance (like a secret rapture) from all of life's pain and disappointments. Regardless of cause or supposed cure, much of the popular end times material—what we could call "pop-prophecy"—will leave one empty.

In contrast, the apostle John serves a rich banquet remarkably different from the fare contemporary end times authors often provide. In Revelation John presents a Lamb who was slain, yet has been raised from the dead and now rules and reigns from His heavenly throne. His power and presence are not confined to heaven, however. In Word and Sacrament He makes Himself truly present in the everyday lives of His holy people. He offers real strength and encouragement in the midst of Satan's assaults, pain, suffering, and death. He has conquered these our greatest enemies; they flee in terror at the sight of His holy cross. He is here, now, with us; He will come again to make everything new. These truly Biblical teachings about God's Lamb can satisfy the hunger of every heart, and soothe the longing of every soul, forever.

This Bible study on Revelation was originally published in 1994. While most of the material remains the same, we have included in this updated version excursuses from the Concordia Commentary series' *Revelation* by Louis A. Brighton and the LCMS Commission on Theology and Church Relations' *The End Times: A Study on Eschatology and Millennialism.* We have also added new or revised Digging Deeper sections at the end of most lessons. These differentiate biblical end times teaching from popular theories including those found in *Left Behind* and similar resources. Also new to this study is a time line sketch of John's life, an outline of Revelation, and an end times glossary.

Bible Study leaders will note the revised chapter titles correspond more easily with chapter headings in Brighton's *Revelation.* For easy reference, the pertinent page numbers of that work are also included at the beginning of each chapter in Leader Notes.

Lesson 1

Revelation and Its Author

With any piece of literature, we want answered The Five W's: *Who? What? Where? When?* and *Why?* This background information not only satisfies our curiosity about the work, but also helps us to interpret it. That is, to a degree these details aid us in understanding the message the author wished to convey to the original reader, and to us. In this lesson we will discuss some of those W's so that we might have a better foundation for understanding the book of Revelation.

Who Wrote Revelation?

1. According to Revelation itself, who is the author (1:1, 4, 9; 22:8)?

2. Look up the following references and write a few brief notes to supply background information about the identity of the author of this book.

a. Mark 1:19–20:

b. Luke 9:28–29:

c. John 13:23:

d. John 18:15:

e. John 19:26–27:

f. John 20:1–10:

g. John 21:1–7:

h. Acts 3:1–10:

3. Had John written this book solely on his own authority, we would rightly hesitate to believe or accept it. It might seem to be merely an account of dreams or nightmares. According to the following passages, by what authority did John write: Revelation 1:1–3, 10–11; 2:7; 14:13; 22:16?

For Whom Was Revelation Written?

In referring to "the seven churches in the province of Asia" (1:4), John seems to indicate that this was a circular letter to be read throughout the Roman province of Asia. The seven churches were located in major cities, and they likely served as centers for the distribution of copies of this letter.

The early Christian church was centered around the eastern end of the Mediterranean Sea. When Revelation was written, Asia Minor was a major center of Christianity. Its six provinces (Asia, Bithynia [including Pontus], Galatia, Cappadocia, Cilicia, Lycia [including Pamphylia]) seem to have been among the wealthiest parts of the Roman Empire at the time. This area of Asia was conquered by the king of Pergamum with the help of the Romans early in the second century before Christ.

The Roman province of Asia was created in 129 B.C. out of the lands bequeathed to the Roman Senate by Attalus III, the last king of Pergamum. It was approximately 300 by 260 miles—an area comparable in size to that of Nebraska or South Dakota. The seven cities addressed in Revelation were centers of wealth, power, and culture.

By the Christian era, Judaism had been well established in Ephesus (Acts 18:19) and presumably in most of the other cities in this province. Christianity was probably first brought to this area by those who on Pentecost had been converted to Jesus Christ (Acts 2:5–11). Paul, the missionary apostle, evidently did not spend much time in the province of Asia until his third missionary journey (ca. A.D. 53–57).

Quite early in their existence these churches needed the encouragement such as that offered by John in Revelation. Already in the early 50s Paul encountered the fanatical devotion of the Ephesian populace to Artemis and the commercial advantage that accrued from this pagan cult (Acts 19:23–41). Soon thereafter, the Roman emperor Nero (A.D. 54–68) made Christians the scapegoat for his own growing unpopularity in the empire. Peter and Paul were victims of the Neronian persecution of the church. A few scholars believe that it was in the face of this persecution that John wrote his letter of encouragement to the Christians in Asia.

However, the majority of scholars believe that this letter was precipitated by the second widespread persecution of Christians in the empire—that initiated by Domitian. It was under Domitian that the cult of emperor worship became widespread throughout the empire. Domitian regarded himself as "Lord and God" and demanded the people's worship throughout his domains. Those who refused were regarded as enemies of the state and were subjected to torture and death. John himself was exiled from Ephesus to Patmos. It was to people in this situation that John penned his epistle.

4. The book clearly identifies the immediate recipients of this letter in Revelation 1:4. These seven churches are identified specifically in Revelation. Look up these verses and write the names of the cities on the map. Refer to the maps in the back of a good study Bible if you need help.

The Seven Churches

Mediterranean Sea

ASIA

Aegean Sea

Patmos

The Purpose of the Letter

A primary purpose of the letter was *to encourage Christians in every age* who must suffer because of their faith in and allegiance to Jesus Christ as their only Lord and Savior.

The overarching theme of Revelation is to unveil for all Christians, including those of first-century Asia, *the reign of God's Lamb upon His throne.* It offers to suffering believers a hopeful perspective of history. Although it seems that Satan and evil rule the universe, God is still in control. Our Savior who lived among us for our redemption has ascended to the Father. There He, with the Father and the Holy Spirit, rules all things both now and forever. Therefore, we can live each moment, in spite of all difficulties, in joy and confidence because our Lord God reigns!

But that is not all. Revelation points us *to a brighter future.* In this book the Lord Jesus reveals to us in a small measure the glory,

14

blessedness, and joy that we can anticipate in a new, eternal age to come. We can greet each day, no matter how dark it may seem, with the assurance of Jesus and the prayer of John, "'Yes, I am coming soon.' Amen. Come, Lord Jesus" (Revelation 22:20).

Revelation is also a *missionary book*. It reveals to us our purpose as Christians in this world. We have been called by God to be His instruments. By the working of His Spirit through the Word, He overcomes the forces of evil in this world and draws people from every nation into the glorious company of His saints.

The placing of Revelation at the end of our Bible is most appropriate. This book is the capstone of all Scripture; it points us to our ultimate, final destiny in which we share with Jesus His eternal exaltation with the Father.

Type of Literature

In his opening words, John identifies his book as an *apocalypse* (revelation, unfolding, unveiling). The word *apocalyptic* is generally used for a writing whose stated purpose is to reveal or unveil the secrets of the future that God has in store for humanity. Apocalyptic literature developed after the exile and has roots in Old Testament prophetic literature, especially Isaiah 24–27 and Zechariah 9–14, along with Joel, Daniel, and portions of Ezekiel. Following are some aspects of apocalyptic literature in general.

1. It is *eschatological* (relating to the end times). It tells of a future period of time when God will break into this world of time and space to bring everything to a final reckoning.

2. It is *dualistic* (presents two opposing principles). It depicts good versus evil, God versus Satan. There are no gray areas—only black and white.

3. It is *pessimistic*. It gives up all hope for peace and righteousness on earth.

4. It is characterized by a *divine plan*. In this plan everything is moving forward according to a predetermined schedule.

5. It uses *pictures, symbols,* and *allegories,* giving special significance to numbers and colors.

6. It is *pseudonymous* (uses a fictitious name). In the nonbiblical apocalyptic literature, the author often claims to be a great figure from Old Testament history who received the message in a vision or

otherworldly journey. Usually an angel interprets the vision for the author or serves as a guide on the journey.

These characteristics especially fit the apocalyptic books that were written between 200 B.C. and A.D. 100. Many of these books are not part of Scripture. They include the Book of Enoch, the Book of Jubilees, the Assumption of Moses, and 4 Esdras. Revelation is different from these apocalyptic books in several important ways:

1. Revelation is *not pseudonymous*; the author of the book is clearly identified (Revelation 1:1, 4, 9; 22:8).

2. Revelation is a book of *prophecy* (Revelation 1:3; 22:7, 10, 18–19).

3. John was *not pessimistic*. Although evil and Satan run rampant in this present age, God is still in control. The exalted Christ is present among His people and rules all things for the ultimate welfare of His followers. The Lamb has obtained for His people victory over Satan, sin, death, and hell (Revelation 12:10–12). In the eternal age to come, God's people will join Christ in His exalted state of perfect joy and bliss.

4. Similarly, John had a *different view of history* than do apocalyptic writers in general. For many such writers the present age is evil and without meaning—a transitory interlude prior to the all-important end of all things. For John this present age that lies between Christ's sojourn on earth and His second coming is a time of God's redemptive activity in history.

Through the proclamation of the Gospel by His people, God is waging a war against the forces of Satan that will culminate with complete victory at the end of this age. In spite of the evil we experience as we fulfill this task, we can be assured of the presence and power of the victorious Lamb to sustain us and give us the final victory.

5. John *did not claim to write merely on the basis of a vision.* He was fully conscious, lifted by the Spirit into a different mode of existence. He not only saw the visions; he experienced them.

6. Although angels play an important role in many apocalyptic writings, *the place of angels in Revelation is distinctive*. Jesus Christ is the angel (the messenger) of this revelation, although He also uses created angels to accomplish His purposes.

16

The Symbolic Language of Revelation

The use of symbols was widespread in the Old Testament world (e.g., Ezekiel), as well as in the Hellenistic world. Although the symbolic language of Revelation causes us some difficulties, the symbols were probably much more readily known to the original readers and hearers. In his commentary on Revelation, Siegbert Becker gives the following helpful information about interpreting symbolic language:

> Symbolic and figurative language must never be pressed beyond the point of comparison. That does not mean that the symbols are arbitrary and can be interpreted any way at all. There is a reason why the Savior is described as a lamb and the devil is pictured as a great red dragon. Those who remember that the Savior told his disciples to let their light shine will know why the seven golden candlesticks are used as symbols for the seven churches. We will have learned how to deal with this book when we have learned to read the Apocalypse the way we read the parables (pp. 15–16).

In the ancient world, grotesque symbols always symbolized something supernatural. Symbols common to everyday life were used to say something about human nature. At times the grotesque was combined with symbols from everyday life to indicate the entry of the supernatural into the normal lives of people (e.g., Revelation 13:17).

When using symbols, a writer usually took entities generally known among his readers so that they could relate to them. Out of this the writer created new meanings. For example, Jews of the first century still regarded the Babylonian captivity with horror, a horror akin to that which the Holocaust holds for present-day Jews. So John used Babylon to represent the satanic power and evil of Rome and also for all future satanic powers that would persecute the people of God.

For Discussion

5. What might the people of God in the world today consider to be their "Babylon"?

6. Give examples of forms of persecution faced by you and the other Christians in your community.

7. Of what promises of God can we remind ourselves in the face of persecution (Romans 8:35–39)?

In Closing

Encourage participants to begin the following activities:
* Read the Gospel of John, chapters 1–2;
* Discuss current events in light of the comforting truths found in John's Revelation;
* Read Revelation 1:1–3:22 to prepare for the next lesson.

Close with prayer.

Lesson 2

John and the Seven Letters

At the very beginning of the Apocalypse, God through John prepared the audience for what would be disclosed. First, John established his credentials and authority for what he was about to describe (Revelation 1:1–20). Second, he prepared his hearers to receive his message with the proper disposition and attitude (Revelation 2:1–3:22). Then, as we shall see in the next lesson, he described the inaugural vision that provides the setting and background for the visions yet to come (Revelation 4:1–5:14).

Prologue and Doxology

8. As you read the prolog to this letter (Revelation 1:1–3), answer these questions:

a. Who is the ultimate source of this letter (1:1)?

b. For what purpose was this revelation given (1:1, 3)?

c. What further information about the theme and purpose of this book is given in 2:10; 22:20?

d. Through whom was this vision revealed to the writer (1:1–2)? According to 1:2, what was it that was revealed to the writer?

e. What probably was the coming crisis ("the time is near," v. 3) for which the writer wanted to prepare the hearers?

9. Read Revelation 1:4–8. Remembering that seven is the symbol for completeness, what might it indicate that God chose seven churches to receive this letter?

10. The three persons of the Trinity are mentioned in verses 4–5. The seven spirits before God's throne is a reference to the Holy Spirit in the fullness of His power and activity. Isaiah 11:2 alludes to the sevenfold gifts of the Spirit.

Recall that three is the number that symbolizes God, and note the threefold structure of what is said about God the Father and about Jesus.

Explain the description of God the Father provided in verse 4 (see also Exodus 3:14).

11. How is Jesus described?

12. What has Jesus done for us and made us (vv. 5b–6)?

13. The world does not now perceive the supreme reign of Christ over all things. When will that become evident to all (see Daniel 7:13–14; Matthew 24:30–31; Acts 1:9–11)?

14. Why will people mourn when Jesus returns? Note the expression of certainty at the end of Revelation 1:7.

15. Commentators do not agree whether the speaker in verse 8 is God the Father or Jesus. In either case, what does it mean that the speaker is the Alpha and the Omega?

16. What comfort do verses 4–8 provide for God's people experiencing persecution?

John's Call to His Prophetic Mission

Read Revelation 1:9–20. In beginning this account of his commissioning, John makes the interesting observation that he shares with his fellow believers "the suffering and kingdom and patient endurance that are ours in Jesus" (v. 9). Even as the divine Jesus reigned also while on the cross, so His people live and reign in and with Him even in the midst of suffering and death.

17. One Lord's Day while in exile on Patmos, John was carried by the Spirit into eternity, where he saw what is and what will be from the view of God Himself. The first thing John heard was a loud voice. What did this voice tell John to do (vv. 11, 19)?

18. When John turned to see who was speaking, he saw one "like a son of man" standing among seven golden lampstands. What was John's reaction to what he saw (v. 17)? What moved John to do this?

19. What reassurance did the figure give John (vv. 17–18)?

20. Although this figure is not named, how do you know it was Jesus?

21. What do the seven stars and the seven golden lampstands represent (v. 20)?

The Letters

Each church faced specific temptations that might lead them away from God—especially in the day of persecution and martyrdom. In these letters Jesus prepared the Christians for impending persecution and assured them of divine power, protection, and blessing. It must be noted that in every generation Christians face similar situations and temptations. They too have the Lord's presence, promise, and protection to see them through.

Each letter is structured around several common elements:

1. Identification of the group being addressed;
2. A description of specific qualities of Christ usually drawn from material in the first chapter;
3. Praise (except for Laodicea) for the church's good record;
4. Identification of the dangers peculiar to that church;

5. A call to repentance;
6. A Gospel promise in the setting of the Last Day.

Ephesus

Ephesus was wealthy and magnificent; it was especially known for its shrine to the Roman goddess Diana (whose Greek name was Artemis). Located on the west coast of Asia Minor, it not only was a major port, but it was also at the center of land routes to the most important cities of Asia Minor. Paul first visited this city about A.D. 52 during his second missionary journey and spent over two years there during his third missionary journey. After his release from his first imprisonment in Rome, Paul likely made several brief visits to Ephesus and left his close friend Timothy in charge of this church (1 Timothy 1:3). One of Paul's best-known letters is addressed to the Ephesians.

John probably went to Ephesus soon after the beginning of the Jewish revolt (A.D. 66). During the reign of Domitian (81–96), John was banished to Patmos where he received his revelation.

Read Revelation 2:1–7.

22. What qualities of Jesus are identified (v. 1)?

23. What good qualities were to be found in this congregation (vv. 2–3, 6)?

24. For what does Jesus reprimand this church (v. 4)?

25. What is the call to repentance (v. 5)?

26. What Gospel promise is given (v. 7)?

27. What applications for today's church do you find in this message to the Ephesian Christians?

Smyrna

Located on an arm of the Aegean Sea, Smyrna rivaled Ephesus as a commercial city. Because of its beautiful setting, it boasted of being the "First City of Asia in beauty and size." It sloped from the sea with its beautiful public buildings located on the rounded top of the hill Pagus. The westerly breeze kept it cool and comfortable throughout the year. The faithful support of Rome by the Smyrnians was proverbial.

Paul seems to have founded the church there during his third missionary journey (A.D. 53–57; see Acts 19:10). Polycarp, a pupil of John, was most likely the head of this church at this time. In A.D. 156, Roman authorities urged Polycarp to say, "Caesar is Lord." He refused with his famous statement, "Eighty and six years have I served Him, and He never did me any injury: how then can I blaspheme my King and my Savior?" Pressed further he finally proclaimed, "You threaten me with fire that burns but for an hour, and after a little is extinguished, but are ignorant of the fire of the coming judgment and eternal punishment, reserved for the ungodly. But why delay? Bring forth what you will." Polycarp expressed in his martyrdom Jesus' encouragement to Smyrna through John, "Be faithful, even to the point of death, and I will give you the crown of life" (Revelation 2:10).

Read Revelation 2:8–11.

28. What does verse 8 tell us about Jesus?

29. What good qualities were to be found here (vv. 9–10)?

30. What special danger might these Christians have encountered in the day of persecution and affliction (v. 10)? Note that the 10-day persecution is symbolic for a complete or intense period of persecution.

31. What words might have been an invitation to repentance?

32. What is the special promise to these believers (vv. 10–11)?

33. What applications to today's Christian would you make?

Pergamum

Because of its location on a huge rocky hill overlooking a great surrounding valley, the Romans made Pergamum the capital of the province Asia. Here the god of healing, Asclepius, was worshiped under the emblem of a serpent—for believers the very symbol of Satan. Many pagan altars, as well as the great altar to Zeus, were located there. As capital of the province, it was also a center for emperor worship with temples dedicated to Caesar. All Christians had to do to remain in good graces in society was to confess publicly, "Caesar is Lord," and offer a grain of incense before Caesar's image as a token of loyalty. Failure to do so meant loss of employment and social status, if not imprisonment and death. Some Christians reasoned, "What harm is there in doing that? We can still in our hearts worship Christ." They wanted to have it both ways—worship Christ in their hearts but worship Caesar in public.

Read Revelation 2:12–17.

34. What description of Jesus is given here (v. 12)?

35. What word of commendation did Jesus have for this church (v. 13)?

36. What word of reprimand did Jesus give (vv. 14–15)? For information about Balaam, refer to Numbers 25:1–3; 31:16.

37. What would happen if the people did not repent (v. 16)?

38. What is the promise (v. 17)?

39. What applications for today do you find?

Thyatira

Situated in a valley connecting two other valleys, this city lacked natural fortifications and therefore was vulnerable to attack. The Romans maintained a strong military base in this city both to defend it and to obstruct the path of those who might seek to follow this easy route to attack the provincial capital, Pergamum. Thyatira was also a center of trade. In view of its character as an army post and a commercial city, vice and immorality were rampant—a constant temptation to the Christians who lived there.

Read Revelation 2:18–29.

40. How is Jesus described in verse 18?

41. What good things did Jesus say about this church (v. 19)?

42. What spiritual danger faced these people (vv. 20–24)?

43. What exhortation to repentance and what encouragement are found in verses 20–24?

44. What words of promise did Jesus offer (vv. 26–29)?

45. How might this message be applied to churches today?

Sardis

At one time this city had been the capital of Lydia, but it had fallen on hard times. The Romans helped it recover some of its former glory. In A.D. 17 it suffered a severe earthquake, but Tiberius helped the city rebuild. Like Thyatira, it was famous for its wool products and its dyeing industry. The Roman system of roads secured for it the trade of central Asia.

Read Revelation 3:1–6.

46. What does verse 1 say about Jesus?

47. What word of praise is to be found in this letter (v. 4)?

48. What condition did Jesus condemn in this church (vv. 1–3)?

49. With what words did Jesus call these people to repentance (v. 3)?

50. What is the word of promise (vv. 4–5)?

51. How might this message apply to Christians today?

Philadelphia

This city was founded by and named after Attalus II (whose devotion to his brother Eumenes gained for him the epithet "brother lover"). It was founded in 138 B.C. as a trade center for the rich volcanic region north of the city. Attalus founded Philadelphia as a center for the spread of the Greek language; therefore it had a certain "missionary" character from its beginning. It was subject to frequent earthquakes. It was a small city; the congregation likely was quite small. Located in a vine-growing region, the cult of Dionysus was predominant. Difficulties for Christians in this city seemed to have arisen more from Jewish opponents than from pagan adversaries.

Read Revelation 3:7–13.

52. How is Jesus described in verse 7?

53. What praise did Jesus have for this congregation (vv. 8–10)?

54. What danger might possibly have faced these Christians whom Jesus commended so highly?

55. How might verse 11 be understood as a call to repentance?

56. What is the Gospel promise (vv. 10–12)?

57. What application for your Christian life and that of the entire church do you find in these words?

Laodicea

Located 40 miles southeast of Philadelphia, this city was founded in the third century B.C. by Antiochus II, who named it in honor of his wife, Laodice. Under Roman rule it became a flourishing commercial center, noted for woolen carpets and clothing. It was a prosperous city, as is evident in 3:17–18. This church was possibly established by Epaphras of Colossae (Colossians 1:7; 4:12–13). At the time of his first Roman imprisonment, Paul had not yet visited the Lycus valley (Colossians 2:1) but seems to have known some of the members by name (Colossians 4:15).

Read Revelation 3:14–22.

58. What description of Jesus is offered in this letter (v. 14)?

59. What praise for this congregation, if any, do you find in this message?

60. What dangers surrounded the members of this church (vv. 15–18)?

61. What is the call to repentance (vv. 18–19)?

62. What is the Gospel (vv. 20–21)?

63. What applications to churches of our time do you find in this message to Laodicea?

In Closing

Encourage participants to begin the following activities:
- Read the Gospel of John, chapter 3–4;
- Discuss the strengths and weaknesses of the seven churches in relation to your congregation today;
- Read Revelation 4:1–5:14 to prepare for the next lesson.

Close with prayer.

Digging Deeper

Numbers and Their Meaning

Numbers figure prominently in Revelation (and a few other books of the Bible), and are often found in apocalyptic literature. Their symbolic use and accompanying interpretation were readily understood by John's readers, but may cause confusion for some Christians when trying to understand his vision. Here are the most common numbers, and their meanings, used in Revelation and other apocalyptic literature:

3—God the Holy Trinity: Father, Son, and Holy Spirit.

4—The world created by God, represented by the four "corners" of the earth, the four winds, the four directions of a compass, and the four seasons.

6—Mankind, created on the sixth day of creation, although because of the Fall this number may also represent sin.

7—Perfection, completeness, holiness. God rested on the seventh day. We are to forgive "70 times 7" times, meaning fully or completely. Seven also represents the Holy Spirit's work among God's people, or God's work in the created world (3 + 4 = 7).

8—Restored creation brought about the Holy Trinity (7 + 1 = 8).

10—Also refers to completeness, and is frequently used in combination with other numbers. There were ten plagues against ancient Egypt. God gave the Ten Commandments to Israel. The Old Testament describes victories over enemies numbering tens of thousands (10 x 10 x 10).

12—Frequently refers to God's people. There were twelve sons of Jacob (and thus twelve tribes of Israel), and twelve apostles.

24—Represents all of God's people of both the Old and New Testaments (12 + 12 = 24).

40—A time of testing and trial. During the Flood rain fell on the earth forty days and forty nights. Israel's wandering in the desert was for forty years. Christ's fasting and temptation in the desert lasted forty days.

1,000—The highest number of completeness (10 x 10 x 10 = 1,000).

Lesson 3

Lamb Enthroned in Heaven

After preparing the readers of Revelation 1–3 to receive the visions to come, John now, in chapters 4–5, describes the setting in which he received his revelation from Jesus and the angels.

Before the Throne of God

Read Revelation 4.

The voice of Jesus in Revelation 1:10–11 invites John to write a scroll to be sent to the seven churches of Asia. Now that voice invites John to step into the court of God to receive the secret plan of God for the world and especially for His people (4:1–2).

64. The Holy Spirit carried John before the very throne of God to receive God's revelation. More than 40 references to God's throne occur in Revelation. What does God's throne symbolize?

65. Exodus 33:20 provides one possible explanation for why the radiance of God is described reflected in precious stones (4:3). Explain.

66. The rainbow, reminiscent of God's promise to Noah, suggests that God in all His power and majesty is also the God of grace and mercy. The 24 elders seated on the 24 thrones surrounding the throne of God (4:4) represent the believers in every era of human history (the 12 tribes of Israel represent Old Testament believers, plus the 12

apostles denote New Testament believers). The white garments denote Christ's righteousness which clothes His people. The gold crowns and the thrones symbolize their royal authority. Although the enthronement of the people of God lies in the future, believers in Jesus already have "one foot in heaven." See Philippians 3:20–4:1 and explain.

The flashes of lightning and peals of thunder, symbolic of the awesome authority, power, and glory of God, remind us of His presence at Mount Sinai when He gave the Law to His people (4:5). The seven lamps are the seven spirits of God and represent the Holy Spirit, who with His sevenfold gifts is active among God's people to enlighten and endow them with heavenly wisdom (Isaiah 11:1–2). (In His Law God condemns us, but by His Spirit through the Gospel He gives us eternal life and salvation.)

Commentators are not certain what the sea of glass represents. Some see it as a barrier that separates us from God's throne (4:6). Our sin prevents us from reaching up to Him. Through the Gospel of Jesus Christ, the Spirit reaches down to us to draw us to God and heaven.

Along with the 24 elders and the seven spirits, four living creatures are before the throne. These creatures are similar to those seen by Isaiah and Ezekiel.

67. Read Isaiah 6:1–7 and Ezekiel 1; 10. Then compare each of the following sets of references. Note the similarities between the vision of John and the visions of Isaiah and Ezekiel.

a. Revelation 4:3 and Ezekiel 1:28

b. Revelation 4:5 and Ezekiel 1:13

c. Revelation 4:6 and Ezekiel 1:5

d. Revelation 4:7 and Ezekiel 1:10

e. Revelation 4:8 and Ezekiel 1:18; 10:12

f. Revelation 4:8 and Isaiah 6:2

An Unending Hymn of Praise

Take a closer look at the continuous hymn of praise sung by the living creatures in Revelation 4:8. Recalling that the number three symbolizes God, note that the hymn has three lines and that each line has three elements—three holies, three titles for God, and three attributes of God.

68. Compare this hymn to that sung by the seraphim in Isaiah 6:3. What does the triple "holy" indicate?

The similarities in both songs of the titles for God is evident in some English translations. The Hebrew of Isaiah 6:3 literally reads *Yahweh Sabaoth*. Some English versions translate this quite literally as "LORD of hosts." This emphasizes God as the commander of the angelic armies. Others translate the phrase as LORD Almighty. The Septuagint (the Greek translation of the Old Testament used by many early Christians) regularly translates *Yahweh Sabaoth* as LORD Almighty, the same phrase used here in Revelation. Both *LORD Almighty* and *LORD of hosts* reflect the majesty and power of God.

69. Now look at the hymn sung by the 24 elders in Revelation 4:11. For what do they praise God?

70. Why is our recognition of God as the Creator of all things so essential for our understanding of the Gospel of Jesus Christ?

The Bible in Revelation

John could use symbolic language and verbal allusions because his first readers and hearers understood them and could make the proper applications.

71. Compare at least three of the sets of references below. Then make a statement about the relationship between the Old and New Testaments.

a. Revelation 4:1; Ezekiel 1:1; Mark 1:10; John 1:51

b. Revelation 4:1; 1 Kings 22:18–19; Amos 3:7; Jeremiah 23:18

c. Revelation 4:2; Isaiah 6:1; 66:1; Psalm 47:8

d. Revelation 4:3; Ezekiel 1:26–28; Psalm 104:2; Genesis 9:16–17

e. Revelation 4:5; Exodus 19:16–19; Psalm 18:6–13

Who Is Worthy to Open the Scroll?

Read Revelation 5:1–5.

What is the scroll? Several theories have been advanced.

Some identify the scroll with the Lamb's Book of Life (see Revelation 3:5; 13:8; 17:8; 20:12, 15; 21:27). Names were written on both sides (writing on the reverse side of papyrus was very difficult) because of the great multitude of the people of God.

Others believe that the scroll is the Old Testament. Here Jesus takes the scroll of prophecy and declares, as He did in Nazareth, "Today this scripture is fulfilled in your hearing" (Luke 4:21).

However, the most satisfactory understanding is that the scroll contains the revelation of those events that John was to communicate. The scroll records God's redemptive plan from Christ's ministry on earth to the plan's triumphal climax, the establishment of a new heaven and a new earth. The scroll was completely sealed (with seven seals) to indicate that it could only be opened by one worthy to do so. No creature was found worthy to open this scroll or even peek inside to see what the future held. Thus John wept.

An elder comforted John by pointing him to the one who was worthy. The elder used two messianic terms familiar to those versed in the Old Testament—the Lion of the tribe of Judah (Genesis 49:9–10) and the Root of David (Isaiah 11:1–10).

"Worthy Is the Lamb"

Read Revelation 5:6–14. Here John is shown what the ascension and enthronement of Jesus looked like in heaven.

The Lion of the tribe of Judah is now pictured as a Lamb. These two descriptions illustrate the striking, unique combination of majesty and humility that characterizes the life of Jesus.

72. How is the Lamb described in the first part of verse 6? What is the significance of Jesus being described in this way (see Isaiah 53:4–7)?

73. In the Old Testament, horns symbolize strength (Deuteronomy 33:17) and political power (Daniel 7:24). What do the seven horns symbolize?

74. What do the seven eyes symbolize?

The Lamb takes the scroll from the hand of God. This symbolizes not only that the Lamb can open the scroll, but that He controls the events recorded there and uses them for the furthering of God's kingdom.

After the Lamb takes the scroll, the four living creatures and the 24 elders break into song. Note that this is a new song occasioned by what the Lamb has brought about.

75. According to their song, why is the Lamb worthy and what has He done?

76. The voices of a great number of angels then join the chorus of praise. What is the content of their song?

77. Why would the great multitudes of angels already confirmed in their eternal bliss be so concerned and joyful about a redemption that pertains to human beings? Before responding, read 1 Peter 1:10–12; Luke 15:10; and Hebrews 1:14.

78. At this point John's vision anticipates the end of time when every creature everywhere will join the song of praise. Why would all created things join the human family in this hymn of praise for the Lamb's great work of redemption? (See Colossians 1:20 and Romans 8:18–22.)

79. To whom is this praise directed? What does this say about the nature of Jesus?

Even as they began this great hymn of praise in 4:8, so the four living creatures also bring it to an end in 5:14.

For Reflection

80. As the Holy Spirit works in the lives of God's people, when do we stand in awe of God's created universe and Christ's redemptive work as did the four creatures and the 24 elders?

81. How might acquiring a greater understanding of and appreciation for God's great works of creation and redemption affect the way we relate to others?

In Closing

Encourage participants to begin the following activities:
• Read the Gospel of John, chapter 5–6;
• Discuss the symbolic description of Jesus in Revelation 5:6 and how this supports a symbolic interpretation of other passages in Revelation;
• Read Revelation 6:1–7:17 to prepare for the next lesson.

Close with prayer.

Digging Deeper

Four Living Creatures

The four living creatures John describes in Revelation 4:6-9 seem to belong to a higher order of angels, and are in the forefront of the angelic host constantly praising God and serving His creation. With their many "eyes" they are fully alert to all that happens both in heaven and on earth. They serve God and mankind with courage and strength (lion), they have patience and strength enabling them to render service (ox), they are intelligent and wise (human face), and they possess swiftness and accuracy as they eagerly obey God (eagle).

The creatures constantly praise God as their Creator, especially for those attributes meaningful to God's people in times of persecution, such as the first readers of John's Revelation. God is *holy*—utterly separate from all created beings. He is *almighty*—able to protect and save His people. He is *eternal*—alone He is the source and basis of all that endures forever.

In his book *Against Heresies* (written ca. A.D. 170), the early church father Irenaeus attacked the false teachings of the Gnostics. In that work Irenaeus also speculated that the four living creatures were the four Evangelists: Matthew (the man), Mark (the eagle), Luke (the ox) and John (the lion). While Irenaeus' interpretation never received status in the church as official dogma, his symbolism as to the identities of these four mysterious beings continues to find expression in the artistry of the church.

See if you can find representations of the four living creatures—the lion, the ox, the human, and the eagle—in your church's paraments, stained glass windows, on a processional cross or crucifix, or on the cover of the Book of the Gospels. Also, locate in the liturgy where we join in the ancient hymn of these four living creatures, singing "Holy, holy, holy" to the LORD, God Almighty.

Lesson 4

First Vision: Seven Seals

We now are ready to receive the first vision of history that will occur. In Revelation we have three visions, each covering the same ground from different perspectives and using different symbols. The first vision comes in the form of seals (6:1–7:17), the second in the form of trumpet blasts (8:6–11:19), and the third in the form of plagues and censers of God's wrath (15:1–16:21).

In addition, twice we will witness the cosmic struggle between Christ and His saints against Satan and all his evil hosts. The first struggle, or grand sweeping view of all things, is described in Revelation 12:1–14:20. The second is described in Revelation 20:1–10.

Each of these visions and both of these grand sweeping views tells us something about what will occur throughout the New Testament era and something about what will occur at the end of history. The first vision deals with tribulations among humankind.

The Four Horsemen

The earliest Christians looked forward to Christ's return within their lifetime to right all injustices and to usher in the new age. Instead, they were greeted with many grim events shaking their belief in Christ's reign. A series of destructive earthquakes shook the world around A.D. 60. The seemingly invincible Roman armies suffered a humiliating defeat by the Parthians two years later.

After fire destroyed Rome in A.D. 64, the Christians were blamed for the catastrophe and were cruelly persecuted. Following Nero's suicide in A.D. 68, the empire suffered from political chaos as four different leaders fought to become emperor. The great city of Jerusalem was destroyed in A.D. 70 after four years of violent bloodshed. Mount Vesuvius erupted in A.D. 79 covering the luxurious seashore cities of Pompeii, Herculaneum, and Stabiae with more than

60 feet of debris. In A.D. 92 the empire suffered a serious shortage of grain.

As they do now, in the midst of all these catastrophes people asked, "Where is your gracious God?" Christians questioned the reign of the living Christ—especially when they endured suffering because of their allegiance to Him. To bolster their trust in the providence, protection, and rule of Christ, John received this first vision of history to share with God's people on earth.

Read Revelation 6:1–8.

There are differing interpretations as to what the white horse represents. Because of the color of the horse, some identify the rider with Christ (see 19:11) or see this as symbolic for the conquest of the Gospel as it is preached throughout the world. But in the context of the other horsemen, it is perhaps best understood as sinful people's conquering spirit, lust for power, and desire to tyrannize other people.

82. What does the red horse and its rider symbolize?

83. What does the black horse and its rider symbolize?

84. What does the pale horse and its rider symbolize?

85. What examples of situations created by each of these four horsemen can you adduce from recent history? from your own life today?

86. Why would a gracious God permit people to endure all of the suffering created by these catastrophes?

The Fifth Seal

Read Revelation 6:9–11.

87. Who is it that John sees under the altar (v. 9)?

88. Why are these souls crying to be vindicated?

89. What response do the souls receive (v. 11)? Of what does this assure them?

The Great Earthquake

Read Revelation 6:12–17.

Suffering and martyrdom will not continue forever. Eventually this age with its evil and death must come to an end, and a new age will dawn. Upheavals in nature point to the great Day of the Lord. Through such upheavals God is present and active in judgment to overthrow the results of human arrogance. Natural disasters are foretastes of God's final judgment on all human pride and rebellion. No one will escape; the entire fabric of society will be affected (6:15). Thus in the sixth seal John sees the end of this world.

90. This section is built on biblical allusions with which the original readers would have been well acquainted. Look up the following Bible passages and note how the end of the world is described in each. Note also the similarities with this section of Revelation.

a. Isaiah 2:12–22

b. Isaiah 24:1–23

c. Isaiah 34:2–4

91. Compare Jesus' description of the last days in Luke 21:8–19, 25–36 with this and the previous two sections.

92. What does Jesus say will happen at the time the great upheavals in nature take place (v. 27; see also Mark 13:26–27)?

93. With what attitude are Christians to prepare for this time (Luke 21:36)?

The Sealing of the 144,000

In John's vision, the seventh seal is yet to be opened. Revelation 8:1, the opening of the seventh seal, introduces the next vision, which depicts the same time period from another perspective. But before John receives that vision, there is an interlude showing John what happens to God's people in the midst of the world's suffering.

Read Revelation 7:1–8.

Four angels of God hold back the four winds of destruction that would ravish the earth and its inhabitants. (The "four winds of the earth" denote the entire world.)

The 144,000 have been sealed to keep them secure in their faith in spite of all evil in the world. They represent all believers in every period of human history (12 for the Old Testament tribes of Israel x 12 for the New Testament apostles x 1,000 for the number of completeness). The sealing does not protect them from physical sufferings or death, but it does ensure their glorious entrance into heaven.

The 144,000 are not only those martyrs who were killed in defense of the Gospel, they also include all believers. Every Christian in one way or another is a martyr; we all give witness to the faith within us, and are tested in various ways. Not only can we be sure that we will be tested, but we can also be certain that God will keep us secure until we have attained our goal.

94. What assurance do each of the following passages provide that God will keep you secure unto heaven, even in times of tribulation?

a. Philippians 1:6

b. 1 Corinthians 1:4–9

c. 2 Thessalonians 3:1–3

d. 1 Thessalonians 5:23–24

e. John 10:27–30

f. 1 Peter 1:3–5

g. Romans 8:26–39

h. Jude 24–25

The Song of Victory

In the first eight verses of chapter 7 John has described the church militant—the people of God in this world—as they struggle against the forces of evil in the power of the Spirit of God. Now, in verses 9–17, he describes the church triumphant—the people of God—with Him in eternal bliss—who during their lifetime triumphed over the forces of Satan.

Read Revelation 7:9–17.

95. How is God's promise to Abraham (Genesis 15:5) fulfilled in this company before the throne?

96. What is the significance of the white robes and palms (see Revelation 7:14; John 12:12–13)?

97. What similarities do you note between Revelation 7:10, 12 and Psalm 98?

98. What blessings can you anticipate as you look forward to your reception into the company of those before the throne of the Lamb (7:14–17)?

In Closing

Encourage participants to begin the following activities:
- Read the Gospel of John, chapters 7–8;
- Give thanks for God's promise of faithfulness to all believers, represented by the number 144,000;
- Read Revelation 8:6–9:21 to prepare for the next lesson.

Close with prayer.

Digging Deeper

Antichrist

Popular end times "prophesy" books such as *Beginning of the End* by John Hagee and *There's A New World Coming* by Hal Lindsey often depict the Antichrist as political leader endowed with satanic supernatural powers. Is an all-powerful world ruler really the Antichrist the Bible warns us about?

The writer of Revelation speaks specifically about the Antichrist—and antichrists—in two of his epistles: 1 and 2 John. The apostle clearly mentions one, final Antichrist, and numerous antichrists, in 1 John 2:18:

> Dear children, this is the last hour; and as you have heard that the antichrist is coming, even now many antichrists have come. This is how we know it is the last hour (see also 1 John 2:22, 4:2–3; 2 John 7).

Scripture indicate there will be a final Antichrist (Greek: "against" or "in the place of" Christ). He will operate within the church (2 Thessalonians 2:4; 2 Corinthians 6:16; Ephesians 2:21; 1 Timothy 3:15), assume divine privileges (Daniel 7:25; 11:36; 2 Thessalonians 2:4), appear to come as Christ (2 Thessalonians 2:8-9), deny Christ and persecute true Christians (1 John 2:22; 4:3, 2 John 7; Daniel 7:25), and will himself be slain by Christ on the Last Day (Daniel 7:13-14, 26; 2 Thessalonians 2:8). Because of the striking similarities between these passages and the papacy, the Lutheran Confessions ascribe the role of Antichrist to the office—and not the man holding it—of the Roman Catholic pope.

Antichrists, like the final Antichrist, deceptively oppose the Son of God through false teaching. Already during John's lifetime Gnostic teachers opposed apostolic doctrine concerning God's Son by denying His birth and death in human flesh (see 1 John 5:6 where the apostle attests the Spirit's witness to Christ coming by "water" and by "blood"). Since John's day, antichrists have continued promoting their unbiblical views within the church, thereby injuring the faith of many Christians. John urges believers to "test the spirits" (1 John 4:1) of all pastors, teachers, and church leaders to see if what they say and do is based on God's Word.

Lesson 5

Second Vision: Seven Trumpets

An old adage, "repetition is the mother of study," emphasizes the importance both of frequent review and of the value of describing a subject in many different ways. At times the way a matter is presented to us will determine whether or not we will understand it. So, in describing to John events occurring between Christ's first coming and the Last Day, the Spirit of God used a variety of revelations and symbols.

The first vision, as described in Revelation 6, focuses on evils and tribulations caused by human sin. We might call this man's inhumanity to man. But in Revelation 7, the Lord assures His people of every generation that He will preserve them in the midst of affliction and persecution. In the age to come they will stand before the throne of God in eternal bliss.

The second vision (Revelation 8:6–9:21, introduced by Revelation 8:1–5) focuses on the evils in nature that cause people to suffer. Not only human sin, but also Satan's forces from hell affect nature and cause human suffering. Yet in the midst of their plight, the people of God continue to witness triumphantly to the grace and glory of God in Jesus Christ, who lived, died, and rose again to earn our freedom from sin, death, and all evil.

Preparation for the Second Vision

Read Revelation 8:1–5. The opening of the seventh seal both concludes the first vision and introduces the second. After the interlude described in Revelation 7, Jesus the Lamb broke the seventh seal. At first nothing happened; there was "silence in heaven for about half an hour" (8:1). According to rabbinic theology, silence preceded great acts of God's revelation and judgment (see the apocryphal books 2 Esdras 6:39 and Wisdom 18:14–15).

49

This was the prelude to the blowing of the seven trumpets announcing God's judgment upon the earth (the number seven indicates the totality of God's judgment). But just as the seals could not be broken until someone was found who was worthy to break them, so the trumpets could not sound until the prayers of God's people reached heaven.

99. What does this imagery suggest about the place of prayer in the reign of Jesus until the Last Day?

100. In Old Testament times, the trumpet was sounded, among other things, to warn people of danger and to call them together in assembly. Read Joel 2:1–2, 11. What does the trumpet herald? Read Joel 2:12–17. What can the people do?

Nature Polluted

Even as the four horsemen depict evils in human relationships that result from sin, so the first four trumpet blasts portray the evils in the natural universe that come from human sin and demonic activity. Read Revelation 8:6–13.

101. As you begin your study of the plagues in nature produced by the sounding of the first four trumpets, look up Romans 8:19–22. What relationship did Paul see between sin and phenomena in nature? What hope for this natural universe did he hold?

102. The first plague (8:7) points to the evil results of sin on land. The second (8:8–9) notes catastrophes caused by sin on the seas. The third speaks of the pollution of fresh water (8:10–11). The fourth

plague affects our sources of light (8:12). Identify recent events that point to such events today.

103. According to Joel 2:30–32 and Acts 2:18–21, how are we to interpret the catastrophic events in nature we observe today? Where can people turn for salvation?

104. How is it significant that only a fraction of nature is consumed by these events (Revelation 8:7–12; see also Zechariah 13:7–9)?

105. Why should God's people not fear these events (see Psalm 46:1–3)?

106. The fourth plague brings darkness. What does darkness symbolize in Amos 5:18–20; Joel 2:1–2; Mark 13:24–26; Isaiah 13:9–13? What is the meaning of darkness in Colossians 1:13?

107. Look up the following passages. What similarity do you find between the plagues of Revelation and those of Egypt?
a. Exodus 9:13–35/Revelation 8:7

b. Exodus 7:14–24/Revelation 8:8–9

c. Exodus 10:21–29/Revelation 8:12

108. How are the 10 plagues in Egypt and the subsequent Exodus, and the plagues in Revelation and the Last Day, similar (see Revelation 1:5–7; 15:1–4; Luke 21:25–28)?

The Assault from the Abyss (The First Woe)

In the transitional verse Revelation 8:13, an eagle or vulture (a symbol of impending destruction and doom, see Luke 17:37; Hosea 8:1) announces even greater woes to befall unbelievers. (The phrase "inhabitants of the earth" is used in Revelation to refer to humanity in hostility to God.) At the sound of the fifth trumpet, John sees the fallen star (probably Satan) given the key to the abyss. Although God does not cause evil, He permits the fallen angels and humankind to experience the results of their sinful actions.

This vision in Revelation 9:1–21 presupposes a close connection between two worlds, both of which God created at the beginning—the world of the spirit as well as the material universe (Genesis 1:1; Colossians 1:16). Demons were also created by God, originally as angels, but in the exercise of their free will they chose to rebel against their Creator and to seek the destruction of all that is good—including the world with its human inhabitants.

Read Revelation 9:1–12. Here John views the growing intensity of the warfare between Satan and his followers against humankind, the creation of God. The abyss is hell as well as the accumulation of evil, to which all people contribute, and by which all people, whether they choose it or not, are affected.

The locusts, which again remind us of the plagues of Egypt that preceded the exodus of God's Old Testament people, will be let loose on earth prior to the final exodus of all of God's people into the new age. These are the demons who injure people rather than vegetation. Their sting is extremely painful (like scorpions). They are extremely intelligent and cunning (human faces), are very destructive (lions' teeth), are well protected (breastplates of iron), and have as their king one whose name means "destroyer" (possibly Satan himself).

However, their power and the duration of their assault upon humankind are limited. This is not yet the final assault of Satan on humankind, or in particular on Christians. God permits harm to come only to those who do "not have the seal of God on their foreheads" (9:4; unbelievers). Moreover, these minions from hell "were not given power to kill them, but only to torture them for five months" (9:5). God limits the effects and duration of this onslaught so that people might see in their suffering the judgment of God on their sin and hear in this trumpet blast the merciful voice of God calling them to repentance and saving faith.

It is possible that this trumpet blast, and the next, herald the unleashing of false teachings with all of their destructive power: the ability to torment people in mind, soul, and, sometimes, body. Jesus warns us that false prophets will appear and deceive many people (Matthew 24:10–11). That may be how these hordes from hell wreak their destruction.

The Reserves Are Brought In (The Second Woe)

Read Revelation 9:13–21. At the sound of the sixth trumpet a cavalry comes to reinforce these demonic enemies of God and humankind. The four angels of destruction, who previously had been restrained for just this time, are let loose upon the enemies of God's people on earth. That the voice came "from the horns of the golden altar" (9:13) suggests that the prayers of God's people have a part to play in this drama. (On this golden altar the angel had offered the prayers of the saints to God [8:3].)

Although the conflict is intensified, again only a portion of humanity is destroyed. This indicates that the era of God's grace is not yet exhausted. Revelation 9:20–21 suggests God's gracious will and purpose in permitting these woes to befall humankind. Humanity's great sin is that of idolatry—worship of self and whatever people themselves produce and do (humanism can be one aspect of this self-worship). This idolatry strengthens the destructive work of the demonic spirits in the world and bears fruit in murders, magic arts, sexual immorality, and theft (9:21).

One of God's purposes in permitting these evils from the satanic forces to occur is to lead unbelievers to repentance and to a saving knowledge of and faith in Jesus Christ, the Savior (9:21). However, these verses also indicate that we are not to expect many to repent. In fact most will continue on their rebellious path against God.

109. What evidence do you see that God has not yet withdrawn His offer of grace, forgiveness, and acceptance from this world?

110. What does all this suggest about why God has placed you in this world at this time and place?

In Closing

Encourage participants to begin the following activities:
- Read the Gospel of John, chapters 9–10;
- Resolve to be more attentive to prayer, especially for those who do not yet know Christ;
- Read Revelation 10:1–11:19 to prepare for the next lesson.

Close with prayer.

Digging Deeper

Modern State and Land of Israel

Christians hold a special place in their hearts for the Jewish people because "salvation is from the Jews" (John 4:22). To them God entrusted His very words and promises (Romans 3:1, 2), and through them He worked out His salvation for all people (Deuteronomy 7:7–9; Psalm 33:12), bringing forth the world's Savior, Abraham's Seed (Galatians 3:16–19). Racism, hatred and prejudice against Jewish people are particularly abhorrent to Christians, who worship the Word in human flesh (John 1:14), who received His flesh from His virgin Jewish mother (Luke 1:26–38), and who offers His flesh and blood in His Supper for the forgiveness of our sins (Matthew 26:26–28).

Appreciation and thankfulness for the Jewish people withstanding, some Christians are lead astray when it comes to the modern state and land of Israel. Basing their beliefs on modern "prophetic" literature such as the *Left Behind* series by Tim LaHaye and Jerry Jenkins, they assume that modern Israel is identical to the Israel of the Bible, and that Israel's ancient lands belong to the modern state by divine right. These Christians also assume that nations are obligated to support modern Israel in all its endeavors because it is "God's nation" whose citizens are "God's people."

In Romans 4:1–12, Paul argues convincingly that Abraham's true descendants are all those who have been justified through faith in his Seed, Jesus Christ. Paul yearned desperately for the conversion of His fellow Jews to faith in Jesus. He indicated that the true Israel is the Israel of faith: those who trust in the Messiah (Romans 9:1–9). This includes both Jew and Gentile (Ephesians 2:11–22; 3:6; Colossians 3:11) who are equal before God through faith (Galatians 3:26–28) and who have been baptized into Christ's one body (Ephesians 4:4–6). It is to this genuine Israel—the church—the new heaven and the new earth are promised (Romans 4:13; Hebrews 11:13–16; 2 Peter 3:13).

Nations and individual citizens may support the modern state of Israel insofar as that country espouses and pursues just policies for all people. But Christians should not be mislead by false teaching as to the identity of the true Israel, and the glorious cosmic promises her citizens have been given through Abraham's Seed, Jesus of Nazareth.

Lesson 6

Scenes in the Interlude

Recall that Revelation 7 was an interlude between the sixth and seventh seals and pictured the church, militant and triumphant. Now we come to an interlude between the sixth and seventh trumpet blasts. This interlude also deals with the church—this time with the church and its mission and final destiny.

One mystery that puzzles many people is this: Why, with the world so evil, does the good God leave His chosen people on earth to suffer affliction at the hands of the enemies of Christ?

In their distress God's people cry out, "How long, Sovereign Lord, holy and true, until You judge the inhabitants of the earth and avenge our blood?" (Revelation 6:10). They pray, "Amen. Come, Lord Jesus" (22:20). Yet the Lord tarries, and His people continue to suffer. For what purpose does He place His people in this world of evil and death and then delay His coming to deliver them?

The visions recorded in Revelation 10 and 11 uncover some of this mystery for us.

The One Who Calls Us

Read Revelation 10:1–6.

Whether or not we fulfill the responsibilities given us often depends on who gives us those responsibilities. In this vision, John sees a "mighty angel" holding a little scroll lying open in his hand. Revelation 10:1–11 suggests that God's people are placed in this world to achieve specific, God-given responsibilities. In this section we are given clues to help us identify the angel and the importance of our mission.

111. Previous to this whom has John seen whose face is like the sun (Matthew 17:1–2; Revelation 1:16)?

112. To what might the rainbow point (Genesis 9:12–17)?

113. Of what would the cloud and legs like fiery pillars remind John's readers (Exodus 13:21–22; 14:19, 24; 40:34–38)?

114. What do clouds symbolize in these passages: Zephaniah 1:15; Psalm 97:2; Daniel 7:13; Matthew 24:30?

115. Who might this angel be?

116. What significance is there in that this giant plants his right foot on the sea and his left foot on the land?

The Purpose and Task for Which We Are Called

Read Revelation 10:5–7. The mighty angel solemnly swears that our years of waiting are over: this age is coming to a close, and the new age is about to dawn. With the blast of the seventh trumpet all that God purposed in His creation, made possible by the blood of the Lamb (Revelation 5:9–10), will be brought to fulfillment.

We would expect the end to come immediately after Revelation 10:7, but the trumpet is not actually blown until Revelation 11:15. The intervening material between 10:7 and 11:15 seems to be an intrusion. But not so.

In the previous revelations concerning the first six trumpets, the vision focused on the evil and misery that will flourish in the world during the New Testament age until the Last Day. Now we are to focus on this period from a different perspective—that of the people of God and their activity in the world. While the focus before was on Satan and the mischievous work of his followers, now the emphasis is on God's activity of divine grace through His people on earth.

Read Revelation 10:8–11.

117. Compare this section with Ezekiel 2:8–3:4. What is Ezekiel commissioned to do? (Note that a more correct translation of Revelation 10:11 is "prophesy again *before* many peoples" [emphasis added].)

118. In what sense is this the commission of the whole church (see Matthew 28:19–20)?

119. What is the meaning of the command to "take and eat" the little scroll?

120. What is the significance of the scroll being both sweet and sour (see Psalm 119:103; Jeremiah 15:16; Ezekiel 3:3)?

121. Why is this mission so urgent (10:7)?

122. According to Matthew 24:14, what will happen before the end of this age?

123. What opportunities do you have today to fulfill your part in this mission of God's people?

Confidence to Confess Boldly

Reflect on your experiences in confessing your faith before other people. What incidences can you recall when speaking of your faith was easy? When was it difficult? When, if ever, did you meet with outright hostility?

The vision of the two witnesses (11:1–13) was given to encourage you especially when you meet with ridicule, hostility, and persecution as you profess your faith and life in Christ.

Read Revelation 11:1–6. John was commanded to measure the temple. This alludes to a vision Ezekiel had 14 years after the destruction of Solomon's temple. In that vision, the prophet watched as a man measured the heavenly temple and the glory of the Lord returned (Ezekiel 40–43). Ezekiel was to relay his vision to his fellow exiles to comfort them with the knowledge that God would rebuild His temple. Because this was an ideal temple, Ezekiel's vision was no doubt a prophecy not only of the rebuilding of the physical temple but of the building of the Christian church as well.

The temple in John's vision represents the true church, that is, all believers (see 1 Corinthians 3:16–17; 2 Corinthians 6:16; Ephesians 2:19–22). The measuring of the temple indicates that these believers

60

will be protected by God even as He permits unbelievers to have some power to attack the church ("trample on the holy city" [Revelation 11:2]). This will occur throughout the New Testament era ("42 months" [11:2]). Although the saints will suffer and even be killed, they will not lose their faith and perish in unbelief.

However, the outer court (the Court of the Gentiles in the Jerusalem temple) was not to be measured (i.e., protected). This represents either the unbelieving pagan world or, possibly, believers who compromise their faith.

The 42 months represent the Gospel age—the period of time from Christ's ministry on earth to the Last Day. 42 months x 30 days per month = 1,260 days, or 3 1/2 years ("a time, times and half a time" in Revelation 12:14). This will be a period not only of Gospel proclamation but also of affliction. This time span symbolizes a limited period of time during which evil is allowed free rein (see Daniel 7:25; 12:7, 11).

Throughout this age the two witnesses will continue to proclaim the Gospel of Christ. The two witnesses refer to all Christian witnesses; two possibly alludes to the disciples who went out two-by-two to witness (Luke 10:1). Or it may indicate the relatively small number of witnesses in relation to the rest of the world. The sackcloth may denote the message of repentance that Christ's witnesses believe and also proclaim so that people will come to faith in their Savior, Jesus Christ. Or the sackcloth may be symbolic of the suffering and mourning these witnesses will experience.

The two lampstands and the two olive trees refer to a vision seen by the Old Testament prophet Zechariah. They symbolize the royal house of Zerubbabel (who led the people after they returned from exile) and the anointed priesthood, both empowered by the Holy Spirit (see Zechariah 4). The lampstands and the olive trees indicate that the whole community of God's redeemed people during this age comprise a royal house of priests to our God and Father (see 1 Peter 2:5, 9; Revelation 1:6; 5:10).

The Word of God proclaimed by His faithful witnesses is one of life or death; "fire comes from their mouths and devours their enemies" (Revelation 11:5; see also Matthew 16:19; 18:18–20; John 20:21–23). It is the Word of Christ that will be the standard of judgment at the

Last Day; those who reject the Gospel thereby bring upon themselves their own condemnation (see John 12:48).

Revelation 11:5–6 alludes to power given to Elijah (1 Kings 17:1; 2 Kings 1:10–11) and Moses (Exodus 7:14–21). Even as God raised up Moses and Elijah to be His witnesses in their respective generations, so in every generation He raises up faithful witnesses to proclaim His message. Even as He empowered Moses and Elijah to perform great marvels in order to accomplish their mission, so He gives His people today power and protection to fulfill their purpose as Christians in an unbelieving world (Revelation 11:6). As surely as Jesus has come to earth to live, die, and rise again to pay for the sins of the world, He empowers us to witness with boldness and confidence the Good News of the salvation He freely offers.

The Church's Final Persecution and Triumph

God has never promised that being and living as a member of His family will be easy in this present age. On the contrary, we can be sure that as Christians we will be called to suffer for our faith in one form or another (John 16:33). Although throughout history the people of God have enjoyed periods of relative calm and success, these periods have alternated with seasons of intense persecution. For example, the early Jerusalem Christians initially were severely persecuted (Acts 8:1). This period was followed by a season of relative peace and acceptance (Acts 9:31). What examples from more recent history can you suggest?

These cycles of persecution and calm will continue until the end, with each cycle foreshadowing the final persecution of the church and its final triumph. Read Revelation 11:7–14. In symbolic language, this section shows us that final persecution and triumph in which the church follows its Lord to death and resurrection.

124. When will this persecution take place (v. 7; see also Matthew 24:14)?

125. Who is the beast and from where does he come (see Revelation 20:1–3)?

126. What does the beast do to the witnesses (i.e., the church)?

127. What does Sodom symbolize (Genesis 18:20–21)? Egypt (Exodus 5:1–9)? Together with the reference to Jerusalem, which crucified its Lord, what do these places symbolize?

128. Why is it significant that people from all over the world gaze on the bodies of witnesses and refuse them burial?

129. Why do the inhabitants of the earth (unbelievers) celebrate the church's death?

130. Three and a half days symbolize a short, evil period of time (probably equivalent to the "short time" of Revelation 20:3). What happens after three and a half days? Compare this to Ezekiel 37:1–14.

131. Why are those who see the church come to life terrified?

Following their being brought back to life, the witnesses are called up to heaven and the inhabitants of the earth begin to experience God's judgment. They have no choice but to acknowledge Him as God of all. But this is only the beginning of the judgment they will experience. As Revelation 11:14 tells us the second woe is past and the third is soon to follow (that occurs in the next section).

The Day of Triumph

Read Revelation 11:15–19. The blowing of the trumpet by the seventh angel introduces the Last Day—a day of triumph for all believers, but a day of judgment and condemnation for all who rejected the mercy of God in Christ (the third woe). The heavenly host declare the triumphal reign of the Lord and His Christ (v. 15). God has always reigned, but now all His enemies are subdued and He reigns eternally without opposition.

The elders, symbolizing God's people of all eras, join in the hymn of thanksgiving to Him who has entered His eternal reign, a reign established by a great demonstration of divine wrath against the defiant anger and hostility of the world (vv. 16–18).

The cosmic disturbances (v. 19) all point to God's just and righteous judgment on His enemies, all the persons and forces of evil and unbelief. But for believers there is an eternal reward (v. 18) and complete access to the presence of God (symbolized by the ark of the covenant [v. 19]). In the Old Testament the ark was the place where God localized His presence among His people. But because of their sin access to the ark was severely restricted. The high priest could enter the Most Holy Place where it was kept only once a year.

At this point the book of Revelation might be concluded. But there is more that God wants to reveal. John now in Revelation 12:1–14:20 will proceed to explain the underlying causes for all the hostility, opposition, and persecution of God's people on earth.

In Closing

Encourage participants to begin the following activities:
- Read the Gospel of John, chapters 11–12;
- Identify one family member, friend, co-worker, or neighbor with whom you could share the Gospel, and then do so with God's help;
- Read Revelation 12:1–17 to prepare for the next lesson.

Close with prayer.

Digging Deeper

Rapture

According to the Bible, the word *rapture* (Greek: "caught up"), refers to event when living believers (along with those who have died in the faith) are united with their returning Lord on the Last Day:

For the Lord himself will come down from heaven, with a loud command, with the voice of the archangel and with the trumpet call of God, and the dead in Christ will rise first. After that, we who are still alive and are left will be caught up together [raptured] with them in the clouds to meet the Lord in the air. And so we will be with the Lord forever. Therefore encourage each other with these words (1 Thessalonians 4:16–18).

Sadly, this passage has been twisted into a scary teaching of a "secret rapture" involving jetliner and automobile crashes and a host of other disasters. In this scheme, Christ rescues adult believers and children under an "age of accountability" from a seven-year tribulation. This unbiblical teaching has been popularized in the *Left Behind* series by Tim LaHaye and Jerry Jenkins.

The secret rapture theory errs in several ways: (1) It twists Paul's words, and other Scripture passages, out of context; (2) It denies the unmistakable return of Christ who, though He arrives suddenly (5:2–4), comes with a "loud command" and a "trumpet call" (4:16); (3) It denies original sin by maintaining that persons will join Christ in heaven without faith; (4) It promises a chance for repentance following Christ's return; and (5) It robs joy from the Christian by focusing on frightening—and somewhat fictional—imagery.

In 1 Thessalonians 4 Paul reassures believers by stating that the souls of those who die in faith are with the Lord, and that when Christ irrefutably returns on the Last Day they will be reunited with their transformed earthly bodies. Those who are alive also will be transformed, and will join Christ and all the saints to live forever in His kingdom. Instead of frightening believers by teaching a "secret rapture," Paul urges us to "encourage one another with these words."

Lesson 7

Woman With Child
and the Dragon

Each of the previous visions in the book of Revelation cover the period between the time of Christ and the Last Day. This was true of the vision of the seven seals (6:1–8:5) and of the blowing of the seven trumpets (8:6–11:19). This time frame is also the subject of the first grand sweeping view recorded in 12:1–14:20.

This overview marks the introduction of the second division of this book. It stands between the first two visions (the seven seals and the seven trumpets) and the remainder of the book. The first 11 chapters form a whole in themselves—after which the book might well have ended.

In Revelation 12:1 the author makes a fresh beginning. Although the theme of the second division is the same as that of the first, the writer pursues new regions of thought and uses symbolic figures that are almost wholly new.

In the first part of Revelation, John pictures the outward struggle between the church and the world. Now, in these next chapters, the underlying cause of this hostility is revealed. It is the age-old conflict between God and Satan, which accounts for the persecution of the church. Through His life, suffering, death, and resurrection, Christ won the crucial battle on behalf of all His people. But the devil still does not give up; he continues his struggle to enslave and destroy all of God's creatures and His creation. All history from the victorious work of Christ on earth to the Last Day is the violent death-struggle between the church and Satan, with God and Christ behind the church.

The actors playing the major roles in this cosmic struggle are introduced in Revelation 12–14. Then, in chapters 15–20, John depicts God's coming in judgment to destroy His enemies once for all. Finally, in chapters 21–22 he describes the eternal future that awaits all the faithful people of God.

Dragon, Woman, and Child

Chapter 12 is really quite fascinating. It is the story of a mother and her child hotly pursued by a vicious dragon. Read Revelation 12:1–6.

To understand this scene, one must be acquainted with its rich symbolism.

132. *Sign* is a word used to denote those great spectacles that occur in human history to point to the consummation of this age. What signs did Jesus tell us would precede the Last Day (Luke 21:11, 25; Acts 2:19)?

133. Although the child represents the Messiah, the woman who bears the child does not stand for Mary. Rather, before giving birth to the child, the woman symbolizes the people of Israel, God's Old Testament church. After the child is born, the woman symbolizes New Testament believers. Explain.

134. Note how the woman is adorned (12:1). Her garment of the sun denotes glory and exaltation. The moon under her feet indicates that the woman exercises dominion. The crown is a symbol of royalty. Remember that the number 12 symbolizes either the people of God in the Old Testament or in the New; the number 24 stands for both together. Here the 12 stars indicate the Old Testament people of God from whom the child was born. After the birth of the child, the woman symbolizes the church.

This sign appearing in heaven indicates that this is how God, from the perspective of eternity, views His people. What does this description suggest about the worth of God's people of both Old and

New Testament eras? How does this differ from the picture that we might have, given only a temporal, earthly perspective?

135. The second person in this scene is the child who is to be born (12:2, 5). This is a clear reference to such passages as Genesis 3:15; Isaiah 7:14; 9:6; Psalm 2:9; Galatians 4:4–5. What do these passages tell you about this child?

136. In Revelation 12:3 another being appears—"an enormous red dragon with seven heads and ten horns and seven crowns on his heads."

Red indicates blood, symbolic of the destruction that the dragon accomplishes in the world. The word *crowns* in 12:3 is a different word in Greek than the one used in verse 1. The type of crown in verse 3 (*diadema*) denotes the kind worn by Persian kings and indicates that the wearer claims to be God. Thus the seven crowned heads point to the dominion that the dragon deceptively wields over the world. However, this is abrogated authority that does not belong to him naturally. It belongs only to God, to Jesus Christ. The 10 horns denote his claim to have power over all aspects of life. According to Revelation 12:9 and 20:2, who is this dragon?

137. The stage is set; the players have been identified. Let us proceed to the drama. This conflict between the dragon and God and His creatures began already in eternity. When God created the heavens (Genesis 1:1), all of His heavenly creatures were good (see Job 38:4–7). In His love, God gave all of His rational creatures a free will. He did not want the angels or human beings to be robots who loved and

trusted in Him because they had no alternative. He gave these beings the freedom to choose.

Not content with being creatures of God, certain angels wanted to be as God. They rebelled against Him to establish their own independence. Since then they have sought to crush the power of God by destroying His creation. Some scholars believe that verse 4, which speaks of the sweeping of a third of the stars out of heaven, is an allusion to this rebellion in the heavenly realm, a rebellion that has its counterpart on earth among humankind. In such an interpretation the third of the stars could indicate the proportion of angels that the dragon took with him in his rebellion against God. What do the following passages indicate about this rebellion in heaven and its consequences?

a. 2 Peter 2:4

b. Ephesians 6:12

c. Jude 6

d. John 8:44

e. 1 John 3:8

Already in Eden the serpent sought to destroy humankind by inducing Adam and Eve to seek to be as God through independence from God (Genesis 3:1–5). In His grace, God promised a Savior, the offspring of the woman who would crush Satan (Genesis 3:15). In the years following, the people of God yearned for this Redeemer. Their long centuries of eager, even painful, waiting were like that of a pregnant woman (Revelation 12:2). But Satan constantly stood before the people of God (the woman) intending to "devour her child the moment it was born" (12:4).

In God's time, Israel, through Mary, brought forth the Savior "who will rule all the nations with an iron scepter" (Revelation 12:5).

This is an obvious reference to Psalm 2:6–9, a coronation psalm that exalts the Messiah and His everlasting rule over all things.

In Jesus' infancy, Satan used Herod in his attempt to destroy the Savior so that he might frustrate God's plan of salvation and thus destroy all humankind. Throughout His ministry Jesus encountered Satan and his temptations designed to deter Jesus from His saving mission. Even Jesus' miracles were part of this struggle between God and Satan.

At the successful conclusion of His saving mission, Jesus in triumph ascended into heaven beyond any further satanic designs (12:5). But the woman (now representing God's New Testament people, the church) continues to live in this world subject to Satan's temptations. However, God has prepared a refuge (the desert, v. 6) for her. This stay in the desert lasts for 1,260 days, or "a time, times and half a time" (Daniel 7:25; Revelation 12:14). This is the period of the present age during which the people of God, surrounded by God's enemies, witness to salvation in Jesus.

138. What memories would this reference to the desert as a place of refuge bring to John's readers? See the passages below for clues.

- Exodus 16:1–10, especially v. 10

- Deuteronomy 8:2–5

- 1 Kings 17:2–6

- 1 Kings 19:2–9

- Matthew 2:13–15

- Hosea 2:14–15

139. What assurances of safety do God's people have in the desert refuge provided for them in this world?

- 1 John 1:3

- 2 Corinthians 13:11–14

140. What do these passages suggest about a primary purpose of congregational life? of the importance of active involvement in a congregation of believers throughout life?

War in Heaven

Read Revelation 12:7–12. This conflict in heaven is not Satan's original rebellion and fall at the dawn of this created universe. Rather, it seems to be the result of the completion of Christ's saving work. It appears that before then Satan had been free to enter the heavenly precincts to lodge accusations against God's people. Indeed, the word Satan means "accuser."

141. What notable examples of Satan accusing the people of God do we have in the Old Testament (see Job 1:6–12 and Zechariah 3:1–5)?

When Christ died on the cross and rose again in our place, Satan was cast out of heaven entirely so that he could no longer accuse the people of God before the Father. Therefore, it is Michael, rather than Christ, who expelled Satan from heaven.

142. Reread Revelation 12:10–12. What is the basis of our confidence and joy before the throne of God?

143. What is the word of warning in this hymn for people still on earth?

144. In what ways does Paul in Romans 8:1, 31–39 offer assurance similar to that found in Revelation 12:10–12?

War on Earth

Although through His victory on the cross Christ conquered Satan and eliminated his right to stand before God to accuse and condemn the people of God, this was not yet the end of the matter. Satan is on earth and earnestly seeks to persecute "the woman who had given birth to the male child," that is, the church (Revelation 12:13). As we learned in Revelation 12:6, God carries away the woman into the desert, the place of refuge. Here the church is sustained in the midst of opposition and difficulties for "a time, times and half a time," the period from the cross to the Last Day.

145. What significance do you see in the similarity between Revelation 12:14 and Exodus 19:3–6, which uses similar phraseology?

146. According to Revelation 12:17, on whom does Satan make war?

147. According to Revelation 12:11, through what do God's people overcome Satan?

148. According to Revelation 12 what kind of experiences can you expect as a Christian in this world? What joy and confidence do you find in this chapter?

In Closing

Encourage participants to begin the following activities:
* Read the Gospel of John, chapters 13–14;
* Knowing your gifts and abilities, inquire how you might use them in service within your congregation;
* Read Revelation 13:1–14:20 to prepare for the next lesson.

Close with prayer.

Digging Deeper

Armageddon

Revelation 16:16 mentions Armageddon, (Hebrew: *har Megiddo*) meaning "the mountain of Megiddo." While the terrain near the city of Megiddo is part of the Mount Carmel range, Megiddo itself possesses only hills. Ancient Megiddo, which dates back perhaps 5,000 years, played a valuable role in military strategy and trade, guarding the route between Mesopotamia and Egypt called the *Via Maris*, or "Way of the Sea" (see Matthew 4:15).

The Valley of Megiddo (also called Jezreel or Esdraelon) has seen many important battles: In 1468 B.C. the army of Egyptian pharaoh Thutmose III defeated the Canaanites; in 1125 B.C. Barak and Deborah were victorious over General Sisera's Canaanites; in 690 B.C. the Egyptians, under Necho II, defeated the Judah's army and killed King Josiah; and in A.D. 1918 British General Edmund Allenby's Egyptian Expeditionary Force defeated the Ottoman Turks.

Some popular end times "prophets" describe in horrific detail a final battle at Megiddo—including a nuclear holocaust—prior Jesus' 1,000-year kingdom, and before Satan's "little season." But was this what John had in mind? Note that John mentions an "assembling" of worldly kings who are defeated by our victorious Christ.

John's "assembling" brings to mind Peter's words in Acts 4:23–30. Quoting Psalm 2:1–2, Peter prays: "Why did the nations rage and the peoples plot in vain? The kings of the earth take their stand and the rulers gather together against the Lord and against His 'Anointed One'" (vv. 25–26). Paul writes: "[God] disarmed the powers and authorities, [and] made a public spectacle of them, triumphing over them by the cross" (Colossians 2:15).

In both passages Peter and Paul are speaking about God's victory over evil through Christ's suffering and death on the cross. The battle against sin, death, and hell has been fought, and victory has been one! What Christ accomplished on that other mountain, Mount Calvary, will be made manifest to all on the Last Day. When our Lord returns, His justice against His enemies will be swift, merciless, and final (19:11-21). Satan, his forces and his followers will be thrown into the lake of fire forever (v. 20).

Lesson 8

Two Beasts and the Conquering Lamb

The Beast from the Sea

Read Revelation 13:1–10. Here John describes his vision of a beast that arises from the sea to assist Satan in his warfare against God and humanity, in particular the church (the woman and her offspring).

The sea with all its turbulence and violent power is an apt figure to depict the agitated condition of sinful humankind and the seething cauldron of national and social life. Out of this sea come those political, economic, and social powers that presume to take the place of God and seek to wield absolute authority over the lives and souls of people.

As the beast emerges, John sees the hideous "ten horns and seven heads, with ten crowns on his horns" (v. 1). Perhaps the seven heads stress the beast's relationship to the seven-headed dragon of chapter 12 from whom this beast receives its power and authority. First-century readers might possibly have seen in this a reference to Rome with its seven hills.

The 10 horns likely represent all anti-Christian governments that will arise and put themselves in the place of God. (Recall that horns symbolize strength and political power.) The 10 crowns on the horns rather than on the heads suggest that these governments gain their position and power by the use of brute force. Here, as in the description of the dragon in Revelation 12:3, the Greek word for crown— *diadema*—refers to the type worn by Persian kings and indicates that the wearer claims to be God. Note also the blasphemous names written on each head of the beast.

As the beast continues to emerge, John sees its body which looks like a leopard, large and fierce, ready to pounce upon its prey. As the beast steps out of the water, John sees that its feet are those of a bear ready to rend and tear. The mouth is that of a lion eager to devour all of God's good creation.

In this chapter we meet an unholy trinity, whose beings are antithetical to the three persons of the Godhead. God the Father gave Jesus all authority in heaven and on earth (Matthew 28:18). Here Satan gives the beast "his power and his throne and great authority" (Revelation 13:2). And both the dragon and the beast receive the worship of people.

But the dragon and the beast—as powerful as they are—have only the authority allowed them by God. God permits the beast to exercise its authority for 42 months, the period of this Gospel age (from the time of Christ to the Last Day [13:5]).

The fatal wound that has been healed (13:3) may be a parody of the wounds of Christ. Jesus died and rose again and still bears the marks of His crucifixion. This beast bears a wound that appears to have been fatal but was not.

This wound also suggests that when one tyrannical power has been subdued, another arises to take its place. So the world will continue to have a series of tyrannical powers until the Lord returns on the Last Day.

149. The ancient seer Daniel had a vision similar to that of John. Compare Daniel 7:1–28 with Revelation 13:1–10. Identify at least three similarities between these two visions.

150. Images used by John in Revelation 13 appear in other parts of the Bible. Identify those images as they appear in the texts below.

a. Revelation 13:1/Isaiah 17:12

b. Revelation 13:2/Daniel 7:6; Hosea 13:7; Habakkuk 1:5–8

c. Revelation 13:2/Proverbs 17:12; Hosea 13:8

d. Revelation 13:2/Psalm 17:12; Hosea 5:14–15; 13:7; 1 Peter 5:8

151. What does Revelation 13:7 say the beast was given power to do?

152. Throughout biblical history tyrannical powers persecuted and suppressed the people of God. Name three such powers and describe how they persecuted God's people. Which power did John have in mind as he wrote Revelation?

153. Name at least one great power in recent times that arose to oppress the people of God. What were some tactics used to suppress Christians?

154. In your opinion, does Satan ever use the government of your country today to suppress Christians? If so, in what ways?

155. Although it is Satan who uses civil government to tyrannize and suppress God's people, God overrules these evil designs and uses them to accomplish His own purposes. According to Hosea 5:14–15 and Revelation 13:9–11, what is one such purpose?

156. Read Acts 5:29; Romans 13:1–7; 1 Timothy 2:1–6; Titus 3:1–2; and 1 Peter 2:11–17. How does the institution of government itself fit into God's care for our sinful world? What is to be your attitude as a Christian toward your government? Is civil disobedience ever justified? Explain your answer.

157. What does it mean to "worship the beast" (Revelation 13:4, 8)?

158. Who worships the beast and who does not (v. 8)?

159. A natural response of sinners is to meet force with force. What does Revelation 13:9–10 suggest about the desirability (or effectiveness) of the church using force to protect itself or achieve its goals (see also Matthew 26:50–54)? What is your opinion about the church encouraging civil government to pass and enforce laws to help the church achieve its goals? If the church is not to use force, what means does it have to fulfill its mission and to protect itself from its enemies (see Ephesians 6:10–20)?

The Beast out of the Earth

Read Revelation 13:11–18, which describes a second beast. In contrast to the first beast that arises from the sea and has a ferocious appearance, the second beast arises from the more familiar land and is less fearsome in appearance.

160. What might be the significance of the beast having two horns like a lamb (see Revelation 5:6)?

161. What characteristic of the beast reveals its true character?

162. Many scholars think that this beast symbolizes false teachers and their human philosophies. What does Jesus warn about false prophets in Matthew 7:15–20?

163. Note that the second beast exercises authority on behalf of the first beast to the end that the people of the world will worship the first beast (Revelation 13:12). In this capacity to which person of the Trinity is the second beast antithetical?

164. How does the second beast deceive? Compare this with Jesus' statement in Matthew 24:23–24.

165. Whom does this beast deceive?

166. What are the consequences for those who refuse to worship the image of the first beast or to receive the mark of the beast?

Although this section does not specifically say to which beast the mark belongs, the relationship of the two beasts would indicate that it belongs to the first beast. This is confirmed later in Revelation (19:19–20). Those who receive the beast's mark do so in a prominent place. The mark symbolizes allegiance to the beast and may be a parody of the seal placed on the foreheads of the servants of God in Revelation 7:3–4.

There have been numerous attempts to identify the symbolism of the number 666, but it is perhaps best to see it as the number of the unholy trinity, each digit of which falls short of the complete number seven. Although the unholy trinity of Satan, worldly tyranny, and false religion claim the place of God, their claim falls short, and they will not prevail in the end.

The Triumph of the Saints

Read Revelation 14:1–5. John was given a vision of the saints in heaven to encourage him and all Christians to persevere in faith by the power of the Spirit in spite of the allurements, temptations, and persecutions in the world. Here we see the Lamb (Jesus) standing on the heavenly Mount Zion.

167. Who are the 144,000 who are with Jesus?

168. Instead of the mark of the beast, what do these people have on their foreheads?

In great joy because of the victory won and in thanksgiving to the Lamb who delivered them, the saints of God join in a new song—new because their residence in heaven with its eternal bliss and peace is a new experience. This song is at once majestic and sublime ("like the roar of rushing waters and like a loud peal of thunder," v. 2) and also lovely, sweet, and tender ("like that of harpists playing their harps," v. 2). This song reflects the experience of having been purchased by the precious blood of the Lamb; therefore only the saints, those who share in this experience, can learn this song.

169. Recalling that idolatry is often pictured as unfaithfulness to God, what does it mean that these saints are virgins (see 2 Corinthians 11:2)?

Rather than following Satan and his beasts, these saints follow the Lamb. They were purchased by Christ and offered as firstfruits—a choice offering—to Himself and the Father. Because of the redeeming, cleansing blood of Christ, these saints now stand blameless before the eternal throne.

The Mission of the Angels

Read Revelation 14:6–13. In His grace and mercy God continues to delay His coming in order that all people might repent of their rebellion against Him and be led to faith in Jesus Christ by the Spirit's operation through the Gospel. In this section, John, in a vision, sees the sending of the angels just prior to the Last Day to warn all people of impending judgment.

The mission of the first angel (14:6–7) is especially to those who in their absorption with the challenges and charms of this world are unconcerned and indifferent about their future and eternal well-being. The mission of the first angel, through God's people on earth, is to call on all humankind to fear God and prepare for the impending hour of judgment.

Through the proclamation of the Law and Gospel, God's people, throughout the ages, until the end of this age, are to call people to repentance and to place their trust for salvation in Jesus Christ alone.

83

The second and third angels warn against placing one's ultimate trust in the things and powers of this age, which are tools Satan uses to mislead humankind away from God and eternal life.

Babylon symbolizes all the enemies of God's people. Like the two beasts of chapter 13, Babylon has led the nations into adultery against God. Here the angel announces that this great enemy has fallen.

The warning of the third angel (14:9–12) seems to be directed to those who place their ultimate trust in the political powers of this world. At the Last Day all human institutions will come to an end. Then it will be obvious for all to see that all ultimate power and good resides in God alone—the God who has revealed Himself in His Son Jesus Christ.

More than that, having in their lifetime spurned the grace of God in Jesus Christ, these people will now be given justice. The angel in 14:10–11 describes what we truly deserve from God because of our rebellion against Him. If we ignore or reject God's offer of grace mediated by the first angel through the church, this is our just reward.

But those who by the Spirit receive and persevere in the grace of God in Jesus Christ, in spite of all earthly obstacles and temptations, can anticipate an eternity of blessedness (14:12–13).

170. According to Jesus in Luke 17:26–30, what is a major cause for people inheriting eternal destruction?

171. Give three examples showing how people in our day demonstrate their indifference to warnings of judgment and to the Gospel. What evidences of complacency, if any, do you detect in Christianity today? How would you overcome this kind of spirit?

172. What are some opportunities that you personally have for being involved in the mission and message of the first angel?

173. Why is it difficult to endure patiently, obey God's commandments, and remain faithful to Jesus (14:12)? Do you think it is more difficult today to persevere than in former ages? Explain your opinion.

The Final Harvest

Read Revelation 14:14–20. As with other cycles of John's visions, this one ends with the Day of Judgment.

174. How does Matthew 13:24–30 help you understand this passage?

175. What does the description of the Son of Man in Daniel 7:13–14 suggest about the Son of Man in Revelation 14:14?

176. What reassurances for your personal life did you receive from your study of Revelation 13–14?

In Closing

Encourage participants to begin the following activities:
- Read the Gospel of John, chapters 15–16;
- Affirm your role as a citizen by keeping yourself informed of governmental issues and by voting regularly;
- Read Revelation 15:1–16:21 to prepare for the next lesson.

Close with prayer.

Digging Deeper

The Roman Imperial Cult and Early Christians

The Roman imperial cult, or state religion, sprang from a pantheistic belief system primarily associated with the gods and goddesses of agriculture and the home. Each of the gods exchanged specific, divine favors for public worship and praise. Through years of military conquest and exposure to other cultures (especially Greece), Rome's pantheon increased greatly. Politically, Rome found it easier to control foreign peoples by absorbing their deities. Spiritually, by appeasing every deity, Rome could secure every divine favor. Therefore, Rome's imperial cult held a contractual agreement with each of the gods: public worship in exchange for divine blessing.

The Roman imperial cult distinguished between state-sponsored religious practices and private faith. State worship ran the gamut between lavish public worship services, complete with ritual animal sacrifice and prayer, to a more informal public offering of incense and prayer to the image of a god or goddess, or (beginning with Caesar Augustus), an image of the Roman emperor. Personal faith in every deity in the Roman pantheon was not required, nor was private worship of every deity in the Roman home. Citizens, however, were expected to participate in state-sponsored cultic rites. Only the Jews were excluded from this rule, due to their persistent, unwavering loyalty to their one, true God. Others who chose not to participate were met with accusations of atheism, often persecution, and sometimes execution.

John evokes images of this corrupt Roman state religion—specifically emperor worship—in Revelation 13:4. The beast of the sea (demonically influenced political power) accepts such false worship. Working in tandem with the beast of the earth (a corrupt spiritual system; Revelation 13:11–18), it persecutes the church, enticing all to worship the dragon (Revelation 13:4). Early Christians would have readily recognized John's reference to the Caesars, the Roman imperial cult, and Satan and his demonic hoard (see 1 Corinthians 10:14, 20–21). By refusing to participate in polytheistic state-sponsored worship and prayer, the early Christians often paid with their lives. They are now among those who have washed themselves in the blood of the Lamb, and follow Him wherever He goes (Revelation 14:4).

Lesson 9

Third Vision: Seven Censers

Like a crescendo, the events depicted in each vision in Revelation move toward the grand climax of Judgment Day. The first vision of earthly events leading to the Last Day (Revelation 6:1–8:5) emphasizes the evils and tribulations caused by human sin, and focuses on the church's being sealed by God in spite of all persecution.

The second vision (Revelation 8:6–11:19) stresses evils in nature, as well as the effect of the devil's forces, that cause human suffering. Yet in the midst of persecution the church witnesses triumphantly to the Lamb who was slain for the salvation of all mankind.

Now the third earthly vision reveals the final judgments of God poured out on humankind. The church in the meantime sings and celebrates God's judgment on the devil's evil forces and thus the ultimate triumph of the Gospel.

The Church Triumphant

John now tells us about the outpouring of God's wrath on all those who steadfastly resist repenting of their sin and turning to the Savior. But before He describes the outpouring of the censers of God's wrath on unrepentant mankind, he describes the glorious state of the faithful saints in heaven.

Read Revelation 15:1–8.

177. What previous sign is implied with "another great and marvelous sign" in 15:1 (see 12:1–3)?

178. What parallel is there between Revelation 15:1–2 and Exodus 14:21–31?

179. Who are those who are "victorious over the beast and his image and over the number of his name" (v. 2)?

180. What similarity do you see between Revelation 15:2–4 and Exodus 15:1–18?

181. What is the "tabernacle of the Testimony" (Revelation 15:5; Exodus 25:8–9; 40:34–35)? What does this figure indicate about the source of the outpourings of the censers that follow?

182. What does the smoke indicate (v. 8)? See Exodus 40:34–35; 1 Kings 8:1, 10–11; Isaiah 6:1–8; and Ezekiel 44:4.

183. What does the gold used for the censers symbolize (15:7)? Why is it significant that the censers were filled with the wrath of God? What does the ascription of eternity to God in this verse suggest about the finality and duration of divine judgment on unrepentant mankind?

Plagues of Nature

Read Revelation 16:1–9. Here we see a strong resemblance to the plagues of Egypt that preceded the exodus (recorded in Exodus 7:14–11:10) as well as to the first four plagues in the trumpet vision (8:6–12).

184. What is affected by the first four plagues?

185. What similarity do you find between Revelation 16:1–9 and Matthew 24:29–31?

186. Who suffers from the first plague?

187. Why is the third plague a just punishment for God's enemies?

188. What does Revelation 16:9 imply about one of the purposes for these plagues?

189. What encouragement, if any, is there in this vision for you to persevere in the faith and to be diligent in witnessing for our Lord and Savior Jesus Christ?

Plagues among the Nations

Read Revelation 16:10–16.

History suggests that there is an ebb and flow in the age-old conflict between the forces of God and those of Satan. But now in John's revelation God's patience is finally exhausted, and the angels continue to pour out the censers of God's wrath. This judgment will occur not only through phenomena in nature, but also in the political sphere.

Just before the Last Day, darkness will cover the kingdom of the beast. This is the beast from the sea introduced in Revelation 13. Great anti-Christian powers in which people placed their trust will collapse totally. This will cause these people enormous suffering, but they will still refuse to repent.

The Euphrates River, subject of the sixth censer judgment, is an allusion to all great powers that oppress and destroy the people of God. Assyria and Babylon—some of Israel's worst oppressors in the Old Testament—were located in the region of the Euphrates. The drying of the waters symbolizes the removal of a barrier that prevents God's enemies from giving full vent to their oppression.

John sees three evil spirits coming from the mouth of the dragon (Satan), the mouth of the beast (the beast from the sea, representing anti-Christian political power), and the mouth of the false prophet (called the beast from the earth in Revelation 13). These demonic spirits perform miraculous signs and gather the leaders of the world for one last battle against God at a place called Armageddon.

Armageddon quite possibly is a reference to the region around Megiddo, a city near Mt. Carmel, where the Israelites overcame their enemies under Deborah (Judges 4:1–5:31) and where Elijah confronted the prophets of Baal (1 Kings 18:16–40). A literal, geographic place is not meant here; Armageddon is a symbol for the final overthrow of evil by God.

In this vision there is no more reference to this force gathered for battle. Perhaps God upstages the battle by bringing the world to an end before it begins. The same sequence will be shown to John again in coming visions.

"Behold, I come like a thief! Blessed is he who stays awake and keeps his clothes with him" (16:15). This statement by Jesus is similar to statements made by Him in the Gospels concerning His second coming (see Matthew 24:42–44). Not only are God's people to be prepared for these last evil days, but they also are to recognize in these catastrophic events the final coming of the Lord.

The End of All Things

Read Revelation 16:17–21. As with the seventh seal and the seventh trumpet, the seventh censer is the end. God's mercy has been exhausted, and He brings this age to a definite conclusion.

190. Note the similarities between the visions of the last trumpet and the final censer.

a. Revelation 11:15 and 16:17

b. Revelation 11:19 and 16:18, 21

191. What does "the cup filled with the wine of the fury of [God's] wrath" (Revelation 16:19) symbolize (see Isaiah 51:17; Jeremiah 25:15–16; Habakkuk 2:16)? Who must drink it? Who drank it for us (see Matthew 26:36–46)?

192. What does Revelation 16:21 indicate about the apparent hardness of heart toward God and His Son that many people bear?

193. Compare Revelation 16:9 with 16:21. Why is repentance mentioned in the first passage, but not in the second?

194. Contrast the curses of the unbelievers in Revelation 16:9, 21 with the praise of the saints in Revelation 15:3.

195. What message of hope for yourself do you find in this section?

In Closing

Encourage participants to begin the following activities:
* Read the Gospel of John, chapters 17–18;
* Discuss God's victory over evil on Mt. Carmel, located near Megiddo (1 Kings 18:16–40) in relation to His victory on Mt. Calvary (John 19:17–30);
* Read Revelation 17:1–18:24 to prepare for the next lesson.

Close with prayer.

Excursus on Resurrection of the Body

Scripture teaches that whatever of man is in the grave (i.e., his body) rises. The identity of the risen body with the body of one's earthly life is implicit in the term *resurrection*. Just as the resurrected Jesus was the same person as the crucified Jesus and was so recognized by His disciples, so also the dead who are raised will be the same persons who formerly lived on earth. A *continuity* exists between the natural body and the resurrection body of the one who is raised.

However, there is also a *discontinuity* between the natural body and the resurrection body of believers. Just as Jesus' resurrected body was a "glorious body," so too the Christian's "lowly body" will be changed to be like Jesus' glorious body (Philippians 3:21). This change of the Christian's body is necessary because "flesh and blood cannot inherit the kingdom of God, nor does the perishable inherit the imperishable" (1 Corinthians 15:50). Because of mankind's fall into sin, the natural body is now subject to the effects of the fall (such as sin, weakness, disease, aging, and death), a situation which will come to an end at the resurrection.

St. Paul's discussion in 1 Corinthians 15 the most complete commentary on the Christian's resurrected body given in the Bible. The apostle presents six contrasts in this chapter:

What is sown corruptible is raised incorruptible. No longer will it be liable to disease or decay.

What is sown in dishonor is raised in glory. No longer will it have the dishonor of being buried, but it will be glorified, radiant, and shining like Christ's glorified body (Philippians 3:21).

What is sown in weakness is raised in power. The weaknesses causing people to tire and need rest will no longer hinder them.

What is sown a natural body will be raised a spiritual body. No longer will it function according to its natural instincts, but it will live completely under the power and direction of the Holy Spirit.

This mortal nature will put on immortality (1 Corinthians 15:53–54). It will no longer be subject to death.

The Christian's body which now bears the image of the man "of the dust" will then bear the image of Christ (vv. 47, 49; see also Romans 8:29 and Colossians 3:10).

Of course, Scripture does not satisfy all of our curiosity about the resurrection (1 John 3:2). It does tell us, however, that the Christian in both body and soul will be glorious and perfect like Christ, no longer subject to the effects of the fall.

Resurrected Christians will be "like the angels" in that they will "neither marry nor be given in marriage" (Matthew 22:30; Luke 20:35–36). However, the similarity is not to be extended to include incorporeity or loss of identity as male and female. Nor are we to believe that certain natural bodily functions will not longer be necessary in the life to come (see 1 Corinthians 6:13).

Christ's resurrection is both the cause and the guarantee of the Christian's resurrection. His resurrection is the "first fruits" of the final harvest, guaranteeing that those who are in Him shall also rise from the dead (1 Corinthians 15:42–49; Colossians 1:18; Romans 8:29). Through baptism the Christian has already been raised to life and is thus assured of the future bodily resurrection (Romans 6:5, 11, 13; Colossians 2:12; 3:1–4). The indwelling of the Holy Spirit, who was given at baptism, is the pledge ensuring the Christian's future resurrection (Romans 8:11, 23; 2 Corinthians 1:22; 5:5; Ephesians 1:13–14). Likewise, the body and blood of Christ in the Lord's Supper are a foretaste of future eschatological blessings (Matthew 26:29; 1 Corinthians 11:26).

Lesson 10

Fall of Babylon

Twice before in his visions John has been assured of the destruction of Babylon the Great (Revelation 14:8; 16:19). This section concentrates on that destruction.

The Prostitute and the Beast

Read Revelation 17:1–18.

An angel holding one of the seven censers tells John that he will be shown "the punishment of the great prostitute, who sits on many waters" (Revelation 17:1). The reference to many waters is an allusion to the city of Babylon, which sat on the banks of the Euphrates and had many canals. (Babylon is described this way in Jeremiah 51:13.) But before John actually sees her punishment, he is shown more about her and about the beast on which she sits.

196. Why is Babylon called a prostitute?

197. What is meant by adultery (see Jeremiah 3:6–10; Ezekiel 16:20–32)?

198. Who commits adultery with the prostitute (Revelation 17:2)?

Babylon

The historical city of Babylon was located on the banks of the Euphrates River. It was the center of a great empire that around 600 B.C. ruled most of the ancient Near East from the Persian Gulf to the Mediterranean Sea. Babylon was used by God to discipline His people for their unfaithfulness to Him. In 605 B.C. and again in 597 B.C., Babylon invaded Judah and carried some of its residents back to the area around Babylon. Finally, in 586 B.C., Nebuchadnezzar, the great Babylonian king, destroyed the city of Jerusalem, including the temple of God and carried even more exiles into captivity. These people were deported to a pagan land where they were always tempted to participate in pagan worship and sometimes were threatened with force if they did not do so (see Daniel 3). The terror and the shame of the Babylonian Exile made it a powerful image in the minds of God's people for centuries to follow. It is easy to see why Babylon is a powerful symbol of the enemies of God's people.

In the years before the exile, God sent prophets to warn His people of their impending doom and to call them to repentance. Even as God's prophets were prophesying that Judah would be taken captive by Babylon, they were also prophesying the destruction of Babylon (Isaiah 21:9; Jeremiah 50–51). Babylon was crushed by Cyrus the Persian in 539 B.C. Cyrus then encouraged the people of Judah to return to their land and rebuild their temple.

Just as the faithful people of God in the Old Testament looked forward to and rejoiced in the coming destruction of Babylon, so God's faithful people in the New Testament era can look forward to and rejoice in the ultimate destruction of all of God's enemies.

There have been numerous attempts to specifically identify the "Babylon" of which John wrote. Certainly in John's day, the powerful, arrogant, pagan Roman Empire, which set itself in the place of God and, at times, persecuted God's people, was an embodiment of Babylon. But in every age God's people face such enemies.

199. What is the condition of the inhabitants of the earth (unbelievers)? What does this condition symbolize?

200. What makes this prostitute so alluring (17:4; 18:3, 9–19)?

201. In her hand the prostitute holds a golden cup from which she offers her lovers the wine that intoxicates them. What is the true nature of the contents of this cup (17:4)?

202. What does the prostitute's title reveal about her (17:5)?

203. What is symbolized in 17:6 (see also 18:24)?

204. What is the extent of this woman's influence (17:15; 18:23)?

205. Compare Revelation 17:3, 8–12 with Revelation 13:1–4. What does the beast on which the prostitute rides symbolize?

206. What is the reaction of earth's inhabitants to this beast?

207. What causes their reaction (17:8; 13:3)? What does this symbolize?

208. Compare Revelation 17:8 with Revelation 4:8. What does this indicate about the beast? From where does the beast come?

209. The beast himself, who had previously been symbolic of all anti-Christian kingdoms, symbolizes an eighth king. What will be the fate of that king?

210. The 10 kings of 17:12 likely represent the complete number of anti-Christian governments (recall that 10 is the number of completeness). Their reign is short ("one hour") and their authority limited. What is the one purpose of these kings and the beast to whom they give their authority (17:13–14)?

211. Jesus, the Lamb of God, our Savior, who lived, died, and rose again for us, will win the ultimate victory over all evil. Why will the Lamb be victorious? Who accompanies Him in victory?

212. At whose hand does Babylon the Great meet her destruction (17:16)? Who is working behind the scenes?

Babylon Has Fallen!

Read Revelation 18:1–24.

John hears the prophetic announcement that Babylon has fallen. While he and his readers know that it will surely happen, it is still to come.

213. What warning is given the people of God in 18:4 (see also 2 Corinthians 6:14–18).

214. When the hour of Babylon's destruction comes, how quickly will she fall (18:8, 10)?

215. Why will those who have fallen under her spell (18:23) mourn her death (18:9–19)?

216. What is the extent of her fall (18:6–8, 21–23)?

217. What should be the reaction of the people of God to Babylon's fall (18:20, 24)? Why?

In Closing

Encourage participants to begin the following activities:

- Read the Gospel of John, chapters 19–21;
- If you don't know already, locate the names of your local, state, and national political leaders, and include them in your daily prayers;
- Read Revelation 19:1–21 to prepare for the next lesson.

Close with prayer.

Digging Deeper

The Prostitute, the Beast, and the Kings

The prostitute sits on the beast. She is supported by the beast (for a time) and works in conjunction with the beast. There is obviously a political aspect to the prostitute herself (see 17:18), so it is difficult to clearly separate her role from that of the beast. But that is not of concern here. What is important is to see that political forces that put themselves in the place of God aid and abet the luring of people into idolatry. Through political support, the works of the prostitute are so deceptive that even the elect may be deceived by her ministrations (17:6–7). Thus, the prostitute is most clearly identified with apostate Christianity.

The imagery of chapter 17 is rather fluid in places. In 17:9 the seven heads represent seven hills, an obvious reference to Rome, which was built on seven hills. The seven heads also represent seven kings (17:10).

One likely interpretation of 17:10 is as follows: The five kings who have fallen represent the Old Testament empires who at one time or another threatened the people of God with annihilation: Egypt prior to the exodus; Assyria which destroyed the kingdom of Israel; Babylon which took the kingdom of Judah into captivity; Persia under Xerxes, who ordered the killing of the people of Judah; and the empire of Alexander the Great that spawned the cruel Antiochus Epiphanes. The sixth king represents the Roman Empire. The seventh had not yet come at the time of John.

Lesson 11

Song of Victory and Second Coming

Recall the great victory for God's people that John saw in Revelation 18. Following that victory, John heard a joyous celebration in heaven. Read about that celebration in Revelation 19:1–4.

Hallelujah means "praise the LORD." According to these verses, why do God's people praise the Lord?

Marriage Feast of the Lamb

Read Revelation 19:5–10. To better understand this section, it is helpful to know something about ancient Jewish marriage customs. First, there was the betrothal (somewhat similar to our engagement but much more binding) performed before witnesses. In this ceremony God's blessing was pronounced on the pair. From that day forward they were regarded as husband and wife (see 2 Corinthians 11:2 where Paul "betrothed" Christians to Christ), although they did not as yet consummate the marriage.

During the interval between the betrothal and the wedding feast, the groom paid the dowry to the bride's father. At the end of this interval there was a procession for which the bride had prepared and adorned herself. Clothed in his best attire and accompanied by his friends (who bore torches and sang), the groom proceeded to the home of his betrothed to receive her and bring her to his own home or that of his parents. Finally, there was the wedding feast which often lasted 7 or even 14 days.

In *More Than Conquerors*, W. Hendriksen describes this celestial wedding thus:

> In Christ *the bride was chosen already in eternity.* Throughout the Old Testament period the *wedding was announced.* When the Son of God assumed human flesh for our

salvation, *the betrothal took place. Christ paid the dowry price* with His substitutionary life, suffering, and death for the salvation of all humankind. *After an interval* (the entire period from Christ's ascension to the Last Day), Christ will return to receive and accompany His bride, the church, *to the heavenly wedding feast.*

218. In the following passages how is the relationship between the Lord and His people compared to that of a bridegroom and his bride?

a. Isaiah 62:5

b. Jeremiah 2:31–32

c. 2 Corinthians 11:2

d. Ephesians 5:25–32

e. Revelation 21:9–10

219. The New Evangelical Translation (NET) translates the latter part of 19:8 in this way: "For the fine linen consists of the verdicts of 'not guilty' pronounced on the believers." Compare this translation with Revelation 7:9–10 and Isaiah 61:10.

220. What is the significance of the phrase that this "fine linen, bright and clean, was given her to wear" (19:8)?

221. What important truth about angels is given in 19:10?

The Victor Receives His Victory

Read Revelation 19:11–21. This section describes the second coming of Jesus to judge the world in righteousness and to destroy His enemies.

222. Who is the rider on the white horse (19:11)? What does the description "Faithful and True" indicate about the character of the rider and whether we can depend on Him? What does the color of the horse symbolize?

223. According to Revelation 19:11–12, what has the rider appeared to do?

224. What is the significance of eyes "like blazing fire" (19:12; see also Revelation 1:14; 2:18)?

225. The Greek word for crown in Revelation 19:12 is *diadema*, the kind worn by Persian kings indicating that the wearer claims to be God. Here the crowns (many of them) are worn by Him who has the right to wear them. What might be the blood in which the rider's robe is dipped (19:13; see also Isaiah 63:1–6)?

226. According to John 1:1, 14; 14:8–10, what does it mean that Jesus is the "Word of God"?

227. What is the sword with which the rider strikes down the nations (19:15; see also Isaiah 49:2; Hebrews 4:12; Ephesians 6:17)?

228. What do the quotation from Psalm 2:9 in Revelation 19:15 and the name of the rider in 19:16 indicate about Him?

229. What does 19:18 indicate about who will be defeated?

230. What encouragements did you find in Revelation 19 to remain steadfast, by the power of the Spirit, in your relationship with Christ?

In Closing

Encourage the participants to begin the following activities:
- Read 1 John;
- Compare Revelation 19:19–21 to Ezekiel 38, especially verses 17–24;
- Read Revelation 20:1–15 to prepare for the next lesson.

Close with prayer.

Digging Deeper

The Enemy's Final Defeat

In Revelation 19:19–21 John is again shown the great army gathered for battle that he saw in Revelation 16:12–21. Here he is shown a different perspective of the same scene—this one focuses on the complete and final destruction of the beast from the sea and the beast from the earth (here called the false prophet). This great army is arrayed to fight against the rider on the white horse and his army. But as in chapter 16, the battle is not described. Perhaps none took place.

What John sees is the victory of the King of kings and the Lord of lords over all earthly kingdoms opposed to Him (the beast of the sea) and over all philosophies and religions—including apostate Christianity (the beast from the earth)—that would lead people away from Christ in whom alone is salvation.

This evidently is the fulfillment of Ezekiel's prophecy concerning the defeat of Gog and his armies. See Ezekiel 38–39, especially 39:17–24 and Revelation 20:7–10.

Revelation 19:21 is especially meaningful. It reminds us that it is the Word of God that judges people. For those who reject Christ and His salvation, the Word of God is the instrument of judgment and eternal destruction, while for those whom the Spirit brings to faith through the Gospel it is the means of eternal life.

Lesson 12

Millennium and Judgment

Because of the attention given by many people recently to millennialism, Revelation 20 is of particular interest. Theories of millennialism are included in this chapter, so it will be useful to closely examine what the Bible says about this topic.

The Millennium

Before examining the various theories of millennialism, it is best to review the classical interpretation of pertinent Bible passages. Then we will be in a better position to evaluate the theories.

In Revelation 20 we have the second grand sweeping view of history from the time of the earthly ministry of Jesus until the Last Day. In several previous scenes, we were shown the defeat of some of God's enemies. In chapters 17–18 we saw the destruction of Babylon. Chapter 19 revealed the end of the two beasts. Now, in Revelation 20, the end of Satan and death are described.

Read Revelation 20:1–10. Verses 1–9 provide the background for the judgment on Satan in verse 10. John sees an angel descend from heaven to bind Satan in the abyss (hell) for 1,000 years (the symbolic number for a complete period of time). The purpose is to prevent Satan from deceiving the nations until the end of this period of time. While Satan is bound, he still is able to influence and tempt human beings. But he does not have free course to deceive the nations and gather them for a final assault against God and His people (Revelation 20:8).

The binding of Satan occurred with the saving life, death, resurrection, and ascension of Christ (see Mark 3:22–27; Revelation 12:5–12; Luke 10:17–18). Prior to that time the nations were under the dominion of Satan. Pagan worship abounded everywhere. Only one nation, the relatively insignificant Hebrew people, had been chosen by God to bear witness to His promises of salvation. Yet even the

Hebrews were more often unfaithful to God than faithful. Acts 14:16 describes that historical situation.

But during the long period during which Satan was loose and the nations generally followed false gods, the Lord encouraged His people with the assurance that when the Messiah came, He would conquer Satan and inaugurate an age in which people from many nations would come to a saving relationship with the only true God.

231. What promise is contained in each of the following passages?

a. Genesis 12:3

b. Psalm 2:8

c. Psalm 72:8–11

d. Isaiah 42:6

e. Isaiah 60:1–3

f. Amos 9:11–12

g. Micah 4:1–2

232. The binding of Satan began with the coming of Jesus of Nazareth into the world and was completed with His death and resurrection. Many passages from the Gospels describe the conflict between Jesus and Satan during Jesus' earthly ministry. Only a few are listed below. What aspect of the binding of Satan do you find in each of them?

a. Matthew 4:1–11; Luke 4:1–13

b. Mark 1:34; 3:20–30

c. Mark 5:1–20

d. Mark 1:21–28

e. John 12:30–33

233. The living and reigning with Christ on the part of the saints is called the first resurrection. Some maintain that since the conversion of the sinner is referred to in Scripture as a resurrection, the first resurrection can be thought of as starting with one's conversion (see Romans 6:1–11; Ephesians 2:4–6; Colossians 3:1). What is the second resurrection (Isaiah 26:19; Daniel 12:2–3; Matthew 24:31; 1 Corinthians 15:42–57; 1 Thessalonians 4:13–18)?

234. What is the second death (Revelation 2:11; 19:20; 20:6, 14; 21:8; Matthew 25:41, 46; 2 Thessalonians 1:8–9)?

Satan's Doom

Reread Revelation 20:7–10. The day of opportunity for the church's worldwide mission endeavors will not last forever. Toward the close of the New Testament era (the thousand years) and just before the Last Day, God will, for a short time (20:3), permit Satan to make one final, all-out attack against His followers.

Satan will go out to deceive the nations; from throughout the world he will gather a force of people who despise the Word of God and reject God's gracious offer of life and salvation through Jesus Christ alone. (For Jesus' description of these days just before the end see Matthew 24:15–31; Luke 21:10–28.) This great uprising of nations will be the last protest against the church. (In Jewish apocalyptic literature, Gog and Magog, which are mentioned in the Old Testament, became symbols for all the forces of evil.)

As we saw in Revelation 16:12–21 and 19:19–21 (where this force gathered for battle is also pictured), no attention is given to the battle itself, if it even occurs. Here fire comes down from heaven and devours the force. Satan, the last great enemy of God and His people, is cast into the fire of hell entirely separated from God and His goodness.

The Great Judgment

Read Revelation 20:11–15. After John sees Satan's final defeat, he is shown another picture of the Last Day. On that day the earth will be completely destroyed and all humankind from every period of history will be raised and judged by Christ. The criterion is "according to what they had done" (20:12). According to this standard, all people will be condemned to eternal death in hell. However, there will be some whose names have been written in the book of life (20:12). These are the people who acknowledged their inability to do God's will and who placed their trust solely in the saving merits, life, and work of Christ. They will be spared the second death and will live with God in eternal bliss (Revelation 21–22).

235. What great comfort is found in Revelation 20:14?

Millennial Theories

236. Why can we anticipate Jesus' second coming and Judgment Day with joy and confidence in spite of our sin and unworthiness (Romans 5:9; Galatians 4:4–5; 2 Timothy 1:10; Hebrews 2:14)?

237. For what purposes has God placed us in this world (Genesis 1:28–29; 2:15; Acts 1:6–8; Ephesians 5:1–21; 1 Timothy 2:1–4; 1 Peter 2:9)?

238. What happens to us at the end of our earthly life (Philippians 1:21–26)?

239. When will Christ's second coming really occur? What will happen to us, His followers, on that day (John 6:40; 1 Corinthians 15:35–57; 1 Thessalonians 4:13–18)?

240. Why is it futile to try to predict the time when Christ will return again (Matthew 24:36, 42)?

241. Can we anticipate an era of general peace and prosperity in this world prior to Christ's second coming? Why or why not (Matthew 24:3–14; 2 Peter 3:3–10)? To what do these optimistic passages refer (Isaiah 2:2–4; 11:6–9; Joel 2:23–32; Zechariah 9:9–10)?

242. Only one New Testament passage (1 Thessalonians 4:13–17) speaks clearly of the rapture. What is the rapture of which this passage speaks?

243. Why can't we state that either all Jews or all Gentiles eventually will be saved (Romans 9:6–8; 11:25–26)?

This chapter is a source of great encouragement when we suffer in one way or another because of our faith. Instead of engaging in idle speculation, one does better to meditate upon its message and derive the comfort and hope to be found there.

In Closing

Encourage the participants to begin the following:
- Read 2 John;
- Discuss how you might winsomely converse with friends or family members believing in the rapture or premillennial dispensationalism, offering them the true hope found in John's Revelation;
- Read Revelation 21:1–22:21 to prepare for the next lesson.

Close with prayer.

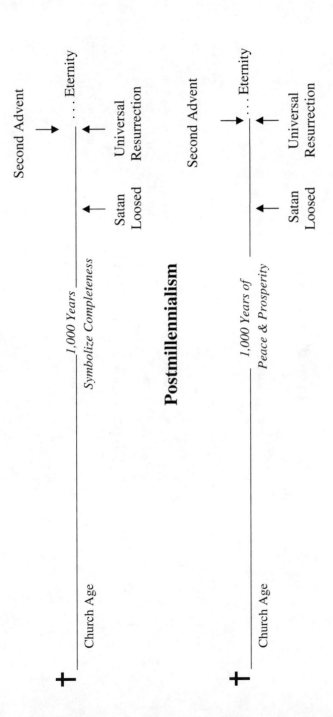

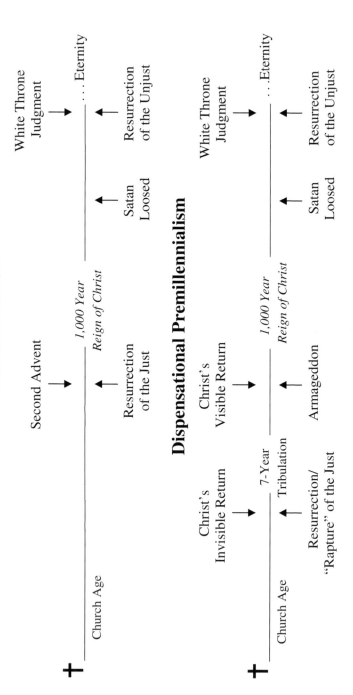

Digging Deeper

Millennium

"A thousand years" appears in the Bible only three times: Psalm 90:4; 2 Peter 3:8; and Revelation 20:4. In the first two passages the phrase refers to *God's timelessness*. But what does "a thousand years" mean in the latter verse? Should it be interpreted literally? The answer to that question determines how other Bible prophecies are interpreted.

There is an interpretation of Revelation 20:4 that agrees with other Bible passages, early Christian teaching, and Reformation theology: Amillennialism (*a*-millennial means *no*-millennium). In this view, Christ's victory on the cross defeated and bound Satan. The "millennial" reign of Christ has already commenced—Christ reigns upon the earth through His church. Yet Christ's victorious saints still fight against evil, including what John calls "the spirit of antichrist" (1 John 4:3). When God has accomplished His gracious purposes in Christ, Satan will be loosed. At that time the Antichrist will appear. Satan's rebellion will be cut off by Christ's glorious return. Then all the dead will rise for Judgment Day. Amillennialism is much simpler than other theories concerning Revelation 20:4, and corresponds better with other Bible passages (particularly Jesus' rejection of an earthly kingdom in John 18:36). It also agrees with the historic Christian creeds. Amillennialism is taught by a majority of Christians, including the Lutheran church.

Other interpretations of Revelation 20:4 include post-millennialism, premillennialism, and dispensational premillennialism. The latter is perhaps the most popular. According to this view, Christ will return and rapture living adult believers, along with those who have not reached an "age of accountability," into heaven. Immediately, a seven-year tribulation period will commence for those on earth. The Antichrist will appear. Christ will return and establish a literal earthly kingdom for 1,000 years. During this time Satan will be bound and certain martyred saints will be resurrected and reign with Christ. After 1,000 years, Satan will lead the nations against God's people in the Battle of Armageddon. Christ will defeat the devil, raise the dead and pronounce final judgment. Millennial theories such as dispensational premillennialism are not supported by the Bible.

Lesson 13

New Heaven and New Earth

If you had your druthers, in what kind of world would you live? People as diverse as Plato (*The Republic*), Thomas More (*Utopia*), and B. F. Skinner (*Walden Two*) have described what they considered to be the ideal society and how it might be attained. You too probably have your view of what a perfect world would be like.

We have a unique description of a perfect world in the last two chapters of Revelation—unique in that this description is based on reality. Here we have a picture of what the world will eventually be like for the people of God—a vision that still lies in the future but which can be partially realized already in this life.

244. In some interesting ways the last two chapters of the Bible and the first three chapters of the Bible parallel and contrast with each other. Note the parallel or contrast in each set of passages below.

a. Genesis 1:1/Revelation 21:1

b. Genesis 1:14–19/Revelation 21:23–25; 22:5

c. Genesis 3:1/Revelation 21:8

d. Genesis 3:8/Revelation 21:3

e. Genesis 3:16–19/Revelation 22:3

f. Genesis 3:22/Revelation 22:14

g. Genesis 3:22–24/Revelation 22:2

As we study this section, as well as other parts of Revelation, we must remember that John wrote of matters beyond our experiences in this world. To enable us to understand the message, the Holy Spirit, through John, used figures of speech that draw on our earthly concepts and experiences. Therefore we need to keep in mind that here we have a spiritual, not a literal, description of the new heaven and the new earth.

A New Heaven and a New Earth

Read Revelation 21:1–8.

245. What does Revelation 21:1 say about the permanence of this present universe (see also Isaiah 34:4, 12; Matthew 24:32–35; 2 Peter 3:10; Revelation 6:14; 20:11–15)?

246. What relationship do you see between Revelation 21:1 and Isaiah 65:17; 66:22; and 2 Peter 3:13?

247. In view of the fact that sin is often defined as alienation or separation from God, what significance do you see in the phrase "coming down out of heaven from God" (21:2)?

248. Note that the new Jerusalem is described "as a bride beautifully dressed for her husband" (21:2). What does the new Jerusalem symbolize?

249. Revelation 21:3–4 interprets the vision of the new creation. To what aspects of this new creation do the following passages point toward?

a. Exodus 25:8

b. Leviticus 26:12

c. Psalm 126:5

d. Isaiah 25:8

e. Isaiah 35:10

f. Ezekiel 48:35

g. 2 Corinthians 5:17

h. 2 Corinthians 6:16

250. How can we—already in this life—experience a foretaste of this bliss?

251. What is promised by God in 21:5? What does God mean when He promises to the thirsty, water without price (21:6; Isaiah 55:1–3; John 4:13–14)? Who is the water of life? What judgment does God pronounce on all those who are not thirsty for this water of life, who reject it?

The Holy City

Read Revelation 21:9–22:5.

Even as one of the seven angels with the seven bowls announced the punishment of the great prostitute Babylon (17:1), so one of the angels with the seven bowls introduced John to the celestial Jerusalem, the holy city of God. The concept of the church being the bride of Christ is frequently used in Scripture (Isaiah 62:1–5; Ephesians 5:25, 32). Several things are said about this celestial city of which we now have a foretaste, but which we one day will enjoy fully and eternally.

It is a city, a community of people—God's people—living together in perfect peace, cooperation, and harmony.

It comes down out of heaven from God (21:10). Our alienation and separation from God will be utterly removed, and we will live in direct, close companionship with Him, the source of all life and joy.

It needs no created luminary. The glory of God gives it light. And its lamp is Jesus Christ Himself, who is all truth and wisdom and who illumines us in all truth and wisdom. Through His Gospel we even now are enlightened in that which is real and true; in heaven we will have perfect understanding (Revelation 21:23–25; Isaiah 60:1, 3, 5, 19–20; John 1:3–5; 8:12).

The city is surrounded by a wall with 12 gates (21:12–13). The high wall denotes perfect safety and security. The 12 gates (three on each side) represent the 12 tribes of ancient Israel. God chose them to be His people to witness to the nations concerning His grace and mercy. Through these gates will pass all those people who have been led to saving faith in Christ. These gates are not to shut people out but are to provide them entrance.

The wall rests on 12 foundations on which are inscribed the names of the 12 apostles (21:14). The church rests on the foundation of the prophets and apostles whose testimony we have in Scripture. The inclusion of both the 12 tribes of Israel and the 12 apostles indicate the continuity and unity of the Old and New Testament people of God—a unity that centers in Christ. (See Ephesians 2:19–20.)

This city is a perfect cube—12,000 stadia in width, length, and height (21:15–17). (This is one possible explanation of the dimensions: 3 [the Trinity] x 4 [the universe] x 10 x 10 x 10 [an indication of ultimate completeness and perfection].) The dimensions suggest the complete, perfect communion we will have with God, only a shadow of which we now experience.

The city is built with most precious stones and pure gold (21:18–21), which suggest the infinite preciousness of this heavenly city. The avenues of pure gold probably also symbolize our absolute purity in heaven, as well as the ready access we have to the throne and to the river and tree of life.

In the new Jerusalem there will be no need for temples and churches; the people of God will fellowship with God directly (21:22).

Believers from every nation will live in this new city. All activity will center in it. All that which is evil will be entirely excluded from it. In this perfect society the gates of the city need not be closed to keep out intruders bent on doing mischief (21:25–27).

This city will be paradise restored (22:1–5). As this universe was created to be paradise, it may be that life in the heavenly Jerusalem will be much like it is here—but entirely without sin and its consequences. Life will be both perfect and eternal.

Jesus Is Coming!

Read Revelation 22:6–21.

252. Why must we take the contents of Revelation seriously (22:6)?

253. Why are we ever to be watchful for the Last Day (22:7, 12, 20–21)?

254. What blessed assurance do we have (22:14, 20–21)?

255. What serious warning must we heed (22:15, 18–19)?

256. What power do we have to enable us to remain faithful in spite of all discouragements, opposition, and temptation (22:17, 21)?

In Closing

Encourage participants to begin the following activities:
- Read 3 John;
- Offer a prayer of thanksgiving to God for His victorious Lamb who is coming soon!

Close with prayer.

Behold, I am coming soon! My reward is with Me, and I will give to everyone according to what he has done. I am the Alpha and the Omega, the First and the Last, the Beginning and the End.

Revelation 22:12–13

Excursus from *Revelation* by Louis A. Brighton

The Lamb of God

The Lamb of God is a beautiful concept that is derived from the Old Testament. Perhaps there is no other description or title of Jesus Christ that so touches the heart of the Christian. Related to it is the idea that Jesus Christ is also the Good Shepherd. Because Jesus was the Lamb of God who was sacrificed for the sins of the people, He became, as a result, their Shepherd. It is not by accident that the twenty-third psalm is possibly the single most quoted chapter of the Bible, for it prophetically draws together what Christ means to His followers. John in his Gospel relates to us how John the Baptist pointed out Jesus as the Lamb of God, who takes away the sins of the world (John 1:29). John's Gospel also describes how Jesus is the Good Shepherd (John 10). Jesus became the Good Shepherd by laying down His life for the sheep (John 10:11). In Revelation Jesus is referred to as both the Lamb of God and as the Shepherd of God's people (7:17).[1]

Both motifs, the Lamb of God and the Good Shepherd, are deeply embedded in the Old Testament. According to the author of Hebrews, the lambs (also bulls and rams) prescribed for sacrifice in the Old Testament were examples or patterns (9:23) of the sacrifice of Christ's death (9:6–10:18). Peter says that Christ, as a blameless and spotless Lamb, redeemed God's people by His blood (1 Peter 1:18–20). That brings to mind the kinds of lambs that were required for sacrifice in the Old Testament (Leviticus 3:1–2, 7–8; 4:32–34; Numbers 6:12). Isaiah prophetically describes how the Suffering Servant carried the guilt of the sheep that had gone astray and was thus led like a lamb to the slaughter (53:5–7; see also Jeremiah 11:19). Ezekiel speaks of Yahweh becoming the Shepherd of His scattered sheep (Ezekiel 34:11–16), and how He will do this by placing over His flock one Shepherd, His Servant, a new David, who would tend and lead the sheep. Thus Yahweh will save His flock (Ezekiel 34:22–24; see also Isaiah 40:10–11; Micah 5:2–4). Throughout the Old Testament God was thus looked upon as the Shepherd of His people (Genesis 48:15–16; 1 Chronicles 11:1–2; Psalm 28:9; 78:52, 70–72; 80:1–2; Jeremiah 31:10–11; Micah 7:14).

In particular, the Passover lamb played an important role in the liturgical and devotional life of the people of the Old Testament. The sacrifice of the lamb and the eating of it initiated the Passover festival. The lamb had to be a year-old male and without defect (Exodus 12:5; Numbers 28:19). Before the Passover meal was eaten the blood of the lamb had to be smeared on the doorframes of the house. The Passover sacrifice and meal were celebrated in commemoration of the deliverance from slavery in Egypt. On the night of the first Passover, as the Passover lamb was eaten, the Lord destroyed the firstborn sons of Egypt. But He passed over the houses of the Israelites because of the blood of the lambs smeared on the doorframes of their homes (Exodus 12:1–30; Numbers 9:1–14; Deuteronomy 16:1–8; 2 Chronicles 35:1–19).

The slaying of the firstborn sons of the Egyptians and the redemption of the firstborn sons of the Israelites (Exodus 13:1–16) could have been a picture of God's promised sacrifice of His own Son for the redemption of the world (see also Genesis 22:1–18). Such an explicit connection is made in the New Testament. Paul in 1 Corinthians 5:7 says that Christ is the sacrificed Passover Lamb. And in the accounts of the Passover meal before Christ's death, there is an apparent connection between Christ's body and blood and His coming death, and the Passover lamb whose blood was shed (Matthew 26:28; Mark 14:24; Luke 22:20). Apart from Paul, however, no other New Testament author explicitly calls Christ the Passover Lamb, but the fact that Paul does so—and does so without explanation—seems to imply that such a connection was widely known. Certainly it was known to the early church fathers, for they often saw in the Passover lamb a type of the sacrifice of Christ.[2]

Of New Testament authors, John makes the most use of the concept of Jesus Christ as the Lamb of God. The Old Testament picture of the lamb and its shed blood introduces Jesus to the public at His baptism (John 1:29, 36). John emphasizes the blood and water from Jesus' side at His death (John 19:34). In 1 John 1:7–9, the blood of Jesus cleanses the sins of those who confess. Together with the water and the Spirit, the blood testifies that Jesus is God's Son (1 John 5:5–9). And in Revelation it is the picture of the Lamb who was slain that is used to introduce the Lord Christ at His presentation to God on His heavenly throne (5:6, 9, 12–13), and it is by the blood of the Lamb that the saints of God also stand before His heavenly Father (7:13–17).

While the Christology of Revelation deals primarily with the exaltation of Jesus Christ and His glorious reign, the foundation for this exalted Christology is the theology of the Lamb of God, who suffered and died and rose again.[3] By this suffering, death, and victory He merited the eternal glory of His Father, the glory He now shares with His people. Throughout Revelation the exalted Christ is the focus of the prophetic message. But also throughout the message of Revelation there is a constant reminder that Jesus Christ is the exalted Son of Man and Lord of lords and King of kings because He was and is the Lamb of God, who was sacrificed for the sins of God's people (1:18; 2:8; 5:6–13; 6:1, 16; 7:9–17; 12:11; 13:8; 14:1–5, 10; 15:3; 17:14; 19:6–9; 21:9, 22–27; 22:1–3).

---

[1] Rev 7:17 states, "The Lamb, who is the midst of the throne, will shepherd them."

[2] Irenaeus, *Against Heresies,* 4.10.1; Justin Martyr, *Dialogue with Trypho,* 40.1; Origen, *Against Celsus,* 8.22. For other references see G. W. H. Lampe, ed., *A Patristic Greek Lexicon* (Oxford University Press, 1961), s.v. *pascha,* 1046–49.
Ancient Jewish writings rarely—if ever—spoke of the sacrificial lamb in reference to the Messiah. Apart from the Testament of Joseph (19:8–11)—and that may be a Christian interpolation (J. Jeremias, *"amnos," TDNT* 1:338)— there seems to be no description of the Messiah as a lamb, though God's people are pictured as sheep and Yahweh as their Shepherd (see 1 Enoch 90). The Testament of Joseph (19:8–11) states that the Savior of Israel will be born of a virgin and will be called the Lamb of God. This Lamb will conquer all the wild animals. The text of the Testament of Joseph can be found in the Testaments of the Twelve Patriarchs (J. Charlesworth, ed., *Pseudepigrapha* [Garden City, N.Y.: Doubleday, 1983], 1:775–828).

[3] Thus also John the Seer is a theologian of the cross.

Leader Notes

This guide is provided as a "safety net," a place to turn for help in answering questions and for enriching discussion. It will not answer every question raised in your class. Please read it, along with the questions, before class. Consult it in class only after exploring the Bible references and discussing what they teach. Please note the different abilities of your class members. Some will easily find the Bible passages listed in this study; others will struggle. To make participation easier, team up members of the class. For example, if a question asks you to look up several passages, assign one passage to one group, the second to another, and so on. Divide the work! Let participants present the answers they discover.

Preparing to Teach Revelation

To prepare to lead this study, read through the Book of Revelation. You might review the introduction to Revelation in *The Concordia Self-Study Bible* or a Bible handbook. Familiarity with the apostle John's other writings—his Gospel as well as 1, 2 and 3 John—would also be helpful in understanding John's writing style and common themes, as well as the historical background. A map of Asia Minor at about the first century A.D. would also help, especially with lessons one and two.

If you have the opportunity, you will find it helpful to make use of other biblical reference works in the course of your study. These commentaries can be very helpful: Louis A. Brighton, *Revelation*, Concordia Commentary series (St. Louis: Concordia Publishing House, 1999); Siegbert W. Becker, *Revelation*, (Milwaukee: Northwestern, 1985); Martin H. Franzmann, *The Revelation to John*, (St. Louis: Concordia Publishing House, 1976); and Leon Morris, *The Book of Revelation: An Introduction and Commentary*, Revised Edition, Tyndale New Testament Commentaries (Grand Rapids: Eerdmans, 1969, 1987). Although it is not strictly a commentary, the section on Revelation in *The Word Becoming Flesh* by Horace Hummel (St. Louis: Concordia Publishing House, 1979) also contains valuable material for the proper interpretation of this biblical book.

Approaches to Interpreting Revelation

Several general approaches to the interpretation of Revelation have been used fairly frequently. The *preterist* approach focuses on Revelation's first-century setting and sees the fulfillment of its major prophecies in the fall of Rome. The *historicist* approach sees Revelation as a forecast of events in human history from the first century until the end of the world. The *futurist* view is that Revelation primarily describes events that will happen near the end of this age. The *idealist* approach regards Revelation as an expression of timeless truths that govern the history of the world and the church.

All of these approaches have something to say to us as we seek to interpret Revelation. It was originally addressed to a first-century situation, but it also deals with events from the time of Christ until the end. We are encouraged to look forward to the Last Day when the victorious Lamb will appear visibly to all humanity to usher in the new eternal age. Certainly, we can discover in this book certain principles that describe how God rules and guides all human history.

As we approach Revelation, it is crucial to note that the book does not proceed in a linear, chronological way from beginning to end, as our Western minds would like. (This point is extremely important to remember when discussing with class participants what they have heard or learned about the end times from non-Lutheran sources.) Like his Hebrew forebears, John uses a cyclical approach in explaining various facets of prophecy. In each of a number of cycles, John reveals (1) something that will occur throughout the New Testament era from the time of Jesus until the end of the world, and (2) something that will occur at the very end. Like television cameras capturing the same touchdown but from different vantage points in a stadium, each prophetic cycle shows the same scene from different angles, emphasizing different things. Each culminates with the end of this age.

Cycles and recurring themes are characteristic of Old Testament literature (e.g., the creation described in two complementary chapters in Genesis 1–2; the poetry of the psalms; Daniel's two visions of the four coming kingdoms in Daniel 2 and 7). John also uses this approach in his Gospel and first epistle (see the outline of these books in *The Concordia Self-Study Bible*).

John makes extensive use of the Old Testament in Revelation. While rarely quoting directly, John creates a mosaic using word

129

patterns, phrases, and thoughts from the Old Testament Scriptures. Your study of this book will be enriched if you make use of the cross-reference section of your Bible, as well as looking up the Old Testament references in this study.

Group Bible Study

Group Bible study means mutual learning from one another under the guidance of a leader. The Bible is an inexhaustible resource. No one person can discover all it has to offer. In any class many eyes see many things, things that can be applied to many life situations. The leader should resist the temptation to "give the answers" and so act as an "authority." This teaching approach stifles participation by individual members and can actually hamper learning. As a general rule don't "give interpretation," instead "develop interpreters." In other words, don't explain what the learners can discover by themselves. This is not to say that the leader shouldn't share insights and information gained by his or her class members during the lesson, or engage them in meaningful sharing and discussion or lead them to a summary of the lesson at the close.

Have a chalkboard and chalk or newsprint and marker available to emphasize significant points of the lesson. Rephrase your inquiries or the inquiries of participants as questions, problems, or issues. This provokes thought. Keep discussion to the point. List on the chalkboard or newsprint the answers given. Then determine the most vital points made in the discussion. Ask additional questions to fill gaps.

The aim of every Bible study is to help people grow spiritually, not merely in biblical and theological knowledge, but in Christian thinking and living. This means growth in Christian attitudes, insights, and skills for Christian living. The focus of this course must be the church and the world of our day. The guiding question will be this: What does the Lord teach us for life today through Revelation?

Teaching the New Testament

Teaching a New Testament letter that was originally written for and read to first-century Christians can become merely ancient history if not applied to life in our times. Leaders need to understand the time and culture in which the letter was written. They need to understand the historical situation of the early church and the social and cultural setting in which that church existed. Such background information can clarify the original purpose and meaning of the letter and shed light on its meaning for Christians today. For this reason, Bible commentaries and other reference works are indispensable when it comes to leading Bible studies.

Teaching the Bible can easily degenerate into mere moralizing, in which "do-goodism" or rules become substitutes for the Gospel, and sanctification is confused with justification. Actually, justified sinners are moved, not by Law, but by God's grace to a totally new life. Their faith is always at work for Christ in every context of life. Meaningful, personal Christianity consists of a loving trust in God that is evidenced in love for others. Having experienced God's free grace and forgiveness, Christians daily work in their world to reflect the will of God for people in every area of human endeavor.

Christian leaders are Gospel-oriented, not Law-oriented: they distinguish between the two. Both Law and Gospel are necessary. The Gospel will mean nothing unless we first have been crushed by the Law and see our sinfulness. There is no genuine Christianity if faith is not followed by lives pleasing to God. In fact, genuine faith is inseparable from life. The Gospel alone gives us the new heart that causes us to love God and our neighbor.

Pace Your Teaching

The lessons in this course of study are designed for a study session of at least an hour in length. If it is the desire and intent of the class to complete an entire lesson each session, it will be necessary for you to summarize the content of certain answers or biblical references in order to preserve time. Asking various class members to look up different Bible passages and to read them aloud to the rest of the class will save time over having every class member look up each reference.

Also, you may not want to cover every question in each lesson. This may lead to undue haste and frustration. Be selective. Pace your teaching. Spend no more than 5–10 minutes opening the lesson. During the lesson, get the sweep of meaning. Occasionally stop to help the class gain understanding of a word or concept. Allow approximately 5 minutes for "Closing" and announcements.

Should your group have more than a one-hour class period, you can take it more leisurely. But do not allow any lesson to drag and become tiresome. Keep it moving. Keep it alive. Keep it meaningful. Eliminate some questions and restrict yourself to those questions most meaningful to the members of the class. If most members study the text at home, they can report their findings, and the time gained can be applied to relating the lesson to life.

Good Preparation

Good preparation by the leader usually affects the pleasure and satisfaction the class will experience.

Suggestions to the Leader for Using the Study Guide

The Lesson Pattern

This set of lessons is designed to aid *Bible study*, that is, to aid a consideration of the written Word of God, with discussion and personal application growing out of the text at hand.

The typical lesson is divided into these sections:
1. Theme Verse
2. Objectives
3. Questions and Answers
4. Closing

The theme verse and objectives give you, the leader, assistance in arousing the interest of the group in the concepts of the lesson. Focus on stimulating minds. Do not linger too long over the introductory remarks.

The questions and answers provide the real spadework necessary for Bible study. Here the class digs, uncovers, and discovers; it gets the facts and observes them. Comments from the leader are needed only to the extent that they help the group understand the text. The questions in this guide, corresponding to sections within the text, are intended to help the participants discover the meaning of the text.

Having determined what the text says, the class is ready to apply the message. Having heard, read, marked, and learned the Word of God, they can proceed to digest it inwardly through discussion, evaluation, and application. This is done, as this guide suggests, by taking the truths found in Scripture and applying them to the world, and Christianity in general, and then to one's personal Christian life. Class time may not permit discussion of all questions and topics. In preparation you may need to select one or two and focus on them. Close the session by reviewing one important truth from the lesson.

Remember, the Word of God is sacred, but this study guide is not. The notes in this section offer only guidelines and suggestions. Do not hesitate to alter the guidelines or substitute others to meet your needs and the needs of the participants. Adapt your teaching plan to your class and your class period.

Good teaching directs the learner to discover for himself or herself. For the teacher this means directing the learner, not giving the learner answers. Directing understanding takes preparation. Choose the verses that should be looked up in Scripture ahead of time. What discussion questions will you ask? At what points? Write them in the margin of your study guide. Involve class members, but give them clear directions. What practical actions might you propose for the week following the lesson? Which of the items do you consider most important for your class?

Consider how you can best use your teaching period. Do you have 45 minutes? An hour? Or an hour and a half? If time is short, what should you cut? Learn to become a wise steward of class time.

Plan a brief opening devotion, using members of the class. And be sure to take time to summarize the lesson, or have a class member do it.

Remember to pray frequently for yourself and your class. May God the Holy Spirit bless your study and your leading of others into the comforting truths of God's Christ-centered Word.

Lesson 1

Revelation and Its Author

Theme verse: *And from Jesus Christ, who is the faithful witness, the firstborn from the dead, and the ruler of the kings of the earth. To Him who loves us and has freed us from our sins by His blood, and made us to be a kingdom and priests to serve His God and Father— to Him be glory and power for ever and ever! Amen.*

Revelation 1:5–6

See Brighton, *Revelation*, pp. 1–29.

Objectives

By the power of the Holy Spirit working through God's Word, we will
- identify the human author of Revelation and the original recipients of this letter;
- describe the circumstances of the original recipients that created a need for this letter;
- identify at least two purposes the author sought to achieve through this letter;
- describe circumstances today similar to those of first-century Christians that make this letter relevant for Christians in our day;
- describe apocalyptic literature;
- demonstrate their understanding of the symbolic language and numbers used in Revelation;
- understand the cyclical structure of Revelation.

This lesson consists of background information necessary for a proper understanding of Revelation. As a class, read through the information carefully, taking time to discuss it as participants wish.

Consult some of the reference materials listed in the study guide for more information on topics of interest to students.

Who Wrote Revelation?

1. The Bible passages clearly identify the writer as John.

2. Some Bible scholars have suggested that the author of Revelation might be John Mark (the writer of the second Gospel; see Acts 12:12, 25; 13:5, 13; 15:37) or a later John the Elder who is not mentioned in the Bible. But the overwhelming view is that this John is John the apostle, the disciple, who also wrote the eponymously titled Gospel and the three epistles that bear his name. This course follows the traditional view that John the apostle authored Revelation. Have participants read through the information given about the apostle John, adding anything else they recall from Scripture.

a. John was the brother of the apostle James. These brothers were the sons of Zebedee and had been engaged in the fishing business with their father. When Jesus called them, they left without delay to follow Him (Mark 1:19–20).

b. John, together with James and Peter, was an eyewitness to the transfiguration of Jesus (Luke 9:28–29).

c. There was a special bond between John and Jesus. John reclined next to Jesus at the Last Supper. John is referred to as "the disciple whom Jesus loved" (John 13:23).

d. Because John was known to the high priest, he was able to follow Jesus into the high priest's courtyard on the night before His death (John 18:15).

e. Jesus gave the care of His mother over to John upon His death, and John took Mary into his home (John 19:26–27).

f. John outran Peter to the tomb on the first Easter morning (John 20:1–10).

g. John was the first to recognize the risen Lord when he appeared to the disciples on the Sea of Tiberias (John 21:1–7).

h. After Pentecost, John was with Peter at the healing of the man at the temple (Acts 3:1–10).

Primary sources for John's later life are Irenaeus (ca. 130–200), especially in his polemical writings against the Gnostics, and Eusebius (ca. 260–340). Tradition indicates that after years of leadership in the Jerusalem church, John moved to Ephesus. This likely occurred sometime shortly after the beginning of the Jewish revolt against Rome in A.D. 66 which culminated in the destruction of Jerusalem (A.D. 70). In the 90s, the Roman emperor Domitian (A.D. 81–96) launched a vigorous persecution of Christians. John was exiled to the island of Patmos, where he wrote the book of Revelation. Upon the death of Domitian, emperor Nerva permitted John to return to Ephesus. Trajan succeeded Nerva in A.D. 98, during whose reign John died. Church father Irenaeus stated that in his old age John was too weak to speak with his former vigor. As John was carried to meetings of the church, he supposedly encouraged the Christians by repeating, "Little children, love one another."

3. Have students look up the listed passages to note the supernatural, divine source of John's visions which he wrote "in the Spirit" (1:10).

For Whom Was Revelation Written?

4. Invite participants to skim the paragraphs that begin this part of the lesson. If time is short, commend the text to their private study and read the last paragraph ("However, the majority of scholars . . ."). Ask students to look up the Bible references to the seven churches in Revelation 2:1, 8, 12, 18; 3:1, 7, 14. Have students locate on the map in the study guide the seven cities addressed by John and the island of Patmos from where he wrote the letter. Refer them to an appropriate map in the back of their Bibles if they need help. Point out the inset on the map that shows the province of Asia in relation to the rest of the Mediterranean region.

The Purpose of the Letter

Throughout history the followers of God have been called on to suffer and die for their faith. This was true already in the Old Testament (see Matthew 5:12; 23:37). Jesus warned His disciples of all eras about the cost of discipleship (Matthew 10:17–39). He Himself was killed by those whom He came to deliver from the tyranny of sin, death, and hell. The first Jerusalem Christians met violent opposition (see the book of Acts). Briefly survey the persecutions of Christians throughout human history. Recall the crass persecution of Christians in the twentieth century in the former Eastern Bloc countries, and the current persecution of Christians in Africa, Asia, and the Middle East. Note also the subtle ways that Christians are persecuted in Canada, Europe, or the United States when they seek to reflect their faith in everyday life. Emphasize that a major purpose of Revelation is to encourage Christians to remain steadfast in their faith in spite of opposition, ridicule, and persecution. A second purpose is to stimulate Christians to be energetic in fulfilling the missionary opportunities of the church in view of the horrendous future that awaits all who reject the Gospel of Christ and in view of the wonderful, blissful future that lies ahead for all the people of God.

Type of Literature

Point out that many people are intimidated by Revelation or misunderstand it because they lack understanding of its distinctive literary qualities and its use of symbolic language and numbers. Note that in the rest of this lesson, students will be introduced to those explanations necessary to properly understand, interpret, and apply this book to their Christian faith and life.

After reading through the information in this section, discuss with your class both the similarities and the differences between Revelation and apocalyptic literature in general.

The Symbolic Language of Revelation

Throughout your study of Revelation, you will encounter a variety of unfamiliar symbols. In the appropriate places these symbols will be explained. But it is desirable for your students at the outset to be prepared to meet with this symbolic language.

Use of such language is rather common today. For example, when someone speaks of the Chicago Bears or the St. Louis Cardinals, we immediately think of a football or baseball team—not animals. So, too, in John's day, people undoubtedly recognized immediately the figures of speech he used. You may think of other examples of symbolic language intelligible to your class that we use today.

For Discussion

5. Examples of "Babylon" in our contemporary world are those governments that persecute Christians. Discuss student responses.

137

6. Though subtle, God's people are persecuted even in countries that permit the free exercise of religion. Examples include the scheduling of sporting events on Sunday mornings, exposure to a media that mocks Christ and His followers, and peer pressure to break God's commandments.

7. God promises His power so that nothing will be able to separate us from His love in Christ Jesus our Lord (Romans 8:35–39).

Numbers and Their Meaning

A major pitfall in the study of Revelation lies in interpreting the numbers found within it. The Digging Deeper section in the study guide describes the symbolism of numbers in Revelation. At appropriate places throughout the course additional information will be given to help you interpret responsibly the numbers as used by John.

Lesson 2

John and the Seven Letters

Theme verse: *Do not be afraid of what you are about to suffer. I tell you, the devil will put some of you in prison to test you, and you will suffer persecution for ten days. Be faithful, even to the point of death, and I will give you the crown of life.*

Revelation 2:10

See Brighton, *Revelation*, pp. 33–102.

Objectives

By the power of the Holy Spirit working through God's Word, we will

- identify three ways John prepared his readers for his message;
- explain the symbolic language used in Revelation 1;
- describe the structure of the letters to the churches;
- discuss the specific circumstances and needs of each of the churches;
- identify the individual message given to each of the seven churches;
- apply the messages to the seven churches to the church of today.

Prologue and Doxology

8. After reading Revelation 1:1–3, discuss the questions in the study guide.

a. The ultimate source is God who, in His Son Jesus Christ, gave this revelation by His angel. The angel was commissioned by Jesus to guide John in his visions of heaven, of earth, of the wilderness, and of the new heaven and new earth (see also Revelation 1:10; 4:1; 10:4, 8; 19:9; 22:8–9).

b. The purpose was to show John and, through him, other believers "what must soon take place." Those who read and heed this prophecy will be blessed, especially when the days of crisis draw near.

c. Christians are encouraged to remain steadfast in spite of persecution (2:10) and to anticipate eagerly the second coming of Jesus (22:20).

d. The angel revealed the visions to John who, in turn, bore witness to the Word of God and the testimony of Jesus Christ that he had received.

e. For John's immediate hearers the crisis likely was the persecutions they were enduring or soon would be enduring. To greater and lesser degrees, every generation since has also faced persecution in its time. Ultimately, the crisis is the great affliction that will precede the second coming of Jesus.

9. In Revelation 1:4–8, we have a beautiful description of the source of all revelation, God. God likely chose seven churches to indicate that His message is for all churches of every time and place.

10. The "who is, and who was, and who is to come" of Revelation 1:4 is the great I AM of Exodus 3:14, the eternal Father, Lord of past, present, and future, the Creator and foundation of all things. All times, past and future, are embraced in His eternal present, which in part will shortly be revealed to John.

11. Jesus, the "faithful witness, the firstborn from the dead" is the martyr par excellence. The Greek word for witness, *martus*, came to be used by the persecuted church to refer to those who witnessed to the truth of God unto death. Hence the meaning of the English word *martyr*. Jesus was a "faithful witness" to the truth of God, and as a result experienced the tyranny of evil in His own suffering and death. But He rose again, becoming "the firstborn from the dead." And He is and always has been "the ruler of the kings of the earth," using them to carry out His purposes.

12. By virtue of His substitutionary life, suffering, death, and resurrection Christ has freed us all from our sins and has made us "a kingdom and priests to serve His God and Father" (Revelation 1:6). This echoes Exodus 19:6 where, after freeing Israel from the tyranny of

140

Egypt, God tells them that they will be for Him "a kingdom of priests and a holy nation" (see also 1 Peter 2:5, 9).

Because of Jesus' atoning work, all believers are part of His kingdom and share in His rule over all nations. Christians are priests not only because they through Christ can approach God directly, but also because through their witness to and proclamation of the Gospel, the Holy Spirit mediates to all people the salvation gained by Jesus.

13. The rule of Christ over all will become evident to everyone when Jesus visibly returns to earth on the clouds to bring this age to a close.

14. Those who have rejected Jesus and His salvation will mourn because finally they will understand their true condition before God as sinful people. They will also see that in rejecting Jesus they have spurned the gracious salvation offered by God and now face only His judgment.

15. *Alpha* is the first letter of the Greek alphabet; *Omega* is the last. Saying that God is the Alpha and the Omega is a way of expressing His control over all of human history. He is before all things and gave them their beginning; He will bring this world to an end.

16. Discuss the comfort that this section gives Christians, especially those who experience persecution and are tempted to doubt that God really is in control. The world does not now acknowledge the reign of Jesus over all things. But a major reason for the giving of Revelation was to enable its readers to see beyond outward circumstances and thus be encouraged by reality as seen from the perspective of God and His angels. At the end, all people will see the eternal realities. But in the meantime, Jesus comes to the world through the Gospel proclaimed by Christians to reveal what is and ever will be.

John's Call to His Prophetic Mission

17. The voice told John to write what he had seen, what is now and what is to happen in the future.

18. John fell as though dead at the figure's feet. Great respect and awe was shown by this action.

19. Jesus told John, "Do not be afraid. I am the First and the Last. I am the Living One; I was dead, and behold I am alive for ever and ever! And I hold the keys of death and Hades" (1:17–18).

20. The appearance of the figure and the sound of His voice all point to the fact that this is Jesus, but the words spoken to John in 1:17–18 confirm that it is He.

This picture of Jesus is rich in Old Testament imagery. In a vision, Ezekiel heard the voice of God, and it too sounded "like the roar of rushing waters" (Ezekiel 43:2). Jesus here resembles an angel whom Daniel saw in a vision (Daniel 10:5–6). In another vision, Daniel also saw "one like a son of man" who received "authority, glory and sovereign power" from the Ancient of Days (Daniel 7:13–14). Interested participants may wish to read Daniel's entire vision in Daniel 7:9–14.

The Ancient of Days (Daniel 7:9–14) is God the Father, and in Daniel's vision He is the one who has white hair. In Revelation, Jesus has white hair. This might be an indication of the fact that Jesus shares the Father's eternal glory and that the Father has given Jesus the authority to rule His kingdom for Him.

Some of the descriptions of Jesus are repeated in the letters of chapters 2–3 and will be discussed in connection with them.

21. The seven stars symbolize the angels of the seven churches. It is not entirely clear who these angels are. Some scholars think that they represent heavenly beings, perhaps the church's guardian angels. But the fact that the letters to the churches are addressed to these angels might indicate that they represent the pastors of the congregations. The seven lampstands are the seven churches themselves. Note that they are only lampstands; Jesus Himself is their light. Be sure that students read the concluding paragraph of this section in the study guide.

Jesus, the Son of Man, is to be found among the lampstands. Although He went to heaven at His ascension to be crowned in glory, Jesus is still present in Word and Sacrament with His angels among His congregations on earth to bless them and finally lead them home into glory.

The Letters

Note the six common elements that appear in the seven letters. Their purpose was to prepare these believers for any trials that might befall them because of their faith, to reassure them of their close relationship with Christ and the hosts of heaven, to sustain and strengthen them in their ordeals, and to encourage them with the assurance that this present age will one day dissolve and that an eternal age of blessedness awaits all of the people of God.

Ask participants to read each letter with these elements in mind.

Ephesus

22. Jesus "holds the seven stars in His right hand and walks among the seven golden lampstands" (Revelation 2:1). Christ rules the angels of these churches (the seven stars) and is present in the midst of these churches (seven golden lampstands).

23. The Ephesian Christians worked hard, persevered in the midst of suffering, and were uncompromising against evil. In their concern for truth, they tested those who claimed to be apostles (who claimed to have been sent by the Lord) but were not. And the Ephesians hated the deeds of the Nicolaitans. We know little about the Nicolaitans, but they seem to have been antinomians (those who are against God's Law). Although they professed to be Christians, they indulged in various immoral practices.

24. Jesus reprimanded this church for forsaking its first love. In their zeal for truth, the Ephesians seemed to have become loveless in their attitudes toward and relationships with one another and Christ.

25. Jesus exhorted the Ephesians to recall what they were like before they forsook their first love, to repent, and to do what they had done before. If the Ephesians failed to repent, Jesus would remove their lampstand. A church may teach the Word faithfully, but in its lack of love may merit Jesus' rebuke.

26. To those who by the power of the Spirit overcome (persevere in faith to the end), Jesus promises the gift of eternal life (v. 7, "to eat from the tree of life").

27. Give students opportunity to apply this message to the church of today. Note that Jesus calls us to love but also to hate evil deeds.

Smyrna

28. Jesus is the First and the Last, the ever-living one who is all in all. He is the one who died and rose again for our eternal salvation and life.

29. These Christians endured poverty (the Greek text indicates extreme poverty), ridicule, and afflictions because of their faith. Yet they remained steadfast in their faith and profession.

30. Eventually these believers might have become so discouraged because of their persecutions that they would have given way to Satan and forsaken the Savior.

31. Possibly the encouragement to remain faithful even unto death.

32. To those who by the power of the Spirit remain faithful unto death, God would give the crown of eternal life. Such people would not be harmed by the second death—eternity in hell.

33. Provide students opportunity to apply this to their lives.

Pergamum

34. Here Jesus "has the sharp, double-edged sword"—probably the Word that is a word of salvation to those who live in Christ, but a word of judgment and condemnation to those who deny or reject Him (v. 12).

35. In the past these Christians had demonstrated their faithfulness to Jesus even when one of their number was martyred.

36. People who held to the teaching of Balaam were tolerated. Balaam was the prophet who was hired by Balak, the king of Moab, to curse the Israelites. The Lord instead had Balaam bless the Israelites. So Balaam suggested to Balak that he entice the Israelites to engage in sexual immorality and Baal worship. Thus they would bring God's judgment on themselves. Evidently there were some in the congregation at Pergamum who advocated indulging in sexual immorality and idolatry. There were also some who followed the Nicolaitans (see the letter to the Ephesians).

37. Unless the church repented of its tolerance of these false teachers and their practices, Jesus would wield the sword of the Law—judgment and condemnation against the false teachers. Part of the church's mission is to call people to repentance and to withhold fellowship from them if they do not repent. The church does no favors to people by tolerating their unrepentant sin.

38. To those who overcome, Jesus will give "hidden manna" (v. 17)—Himself, the bread of life (John 6:33, 35)—and a "white stone." We don't know for sure exactly what this white stone symbolizes, but

perhaps holiness, beauty, forgiveness, and glory that will endure forever. In biblical times, a person's name represented his or her character. When God gives us a new name, He is giving us a new character.

39. Many applications can be given in an age when many people advocate and are involved in immorality and idolatry. Some even seek to be identified with God and the church and yet pursue self-fulfillment regardless of the divine will.

Thyatira

40. Jesus' "eyes are like blazing fire," symbolizing His righteous indignation because of what He in His omniscience knows to be amiss (v. 18). His "feet are like burnished bronze"; He would stamp out all enemies of the truth.

41. Jesus noted their deeds, love, faith, service, and perseverance—and the fact that they had improved since they first came to faith.

42. Jezebel was the wife of King Ahab of Israel. She led many of God's people to sin by advocating the worship of Baal (1 Kings 16:31; 18:19). Like Jezebel, a prominent woman in this congregation was misleading people by advocating sexual immorality and eating meat offered to idols. She also promoted a kind of deep, secret "knowledge," perhaps an early form of Gnosticism.

43. This section (2:20–24) is an obvious call for those who followed the teachings of this woman to repent. Those not following her teachings were encouraged to hold on to what they had.

44. Jesus promises those remaining faithful that they will rule with Him in the age to come. The reference to the morning star is unclear, but we can be sure that it is a precious gift that our Lord promises to those whose faith endures.

45. Encourage students to discuss applications to today.

Sardis

46. Jesus sends the sevenfold Spirit of God, upon whom our Christian faith and life depend, to guide and empower His church. He also sends the angels, or ministers, of His church (the "stars"; see 1:20).

47. In spite of the deadness of this church, a few people were still faithful to Christ.

48. This church was dead. The people went through the motions of religion, but Jesus meant little to them.

49. "Remember, therefore, what you have received and heard; obey it, and repent" (3:3). If they did not, Christ would unexpectantly come to bring judgment on them.

50. Christ acknowledged the few who remained spiritually alive and promised that they would walk with Him, dressed in white, symbolic of His righteousness. To all who overcome, Christ promises this white garment and that their names will never be removed from the book of life. They will inherit eternal life, and Jesus will acknowledge them before His Father and the hosts of heaven.

51. Students will likely be able to cite examples of spiritual deadness today.

Philadelphia

52. "Holy and true" (v. 7) echoes the divine title *Holy One* (see Isaiah 40:25; Habakkuk 3:3; Mark 1:24). Jesus "holds the key of David"—He is the fulfillment of all the Old Testament messianic promises (v. 7). He holds the keys to the kingdom; it is only through Him that a person enters the family of God.

53. In spite of their weakness, these Christians kept Jesus' Word and remained faithful to Him while being opposed by unbelieving Jews.

54. The "open door" in 3:8 may refer to the door of the kingdom or to the door of opportunity to witness for Jesus. If the latter is the case, the danger faced by the congregation may have been that they would not go through that door, that is, they may not have been as alive to their evangelistic opportunities as they could have been.

55. Jesus reminded the people that, in spite of their faithfulness, they too were susceptible to falling away. He warned them against a sense of false security.

56. Jesus promised to keep them safe in the hour of trial and promised those who endured that they would be pillars in the temple of heaven in which they would dwell securely forever. They would belong to God (bear His name), be citizens of His kingdom (bear the

name of the new Jerusalem), and share in the glory of Christ's new, exalted name.

57. Encourage students to discuss applications to today.

Laodicea

58. Here Jesus is called "the Amen, the faithful and true witness" (v. 14). He is the truth and witnesses to God's truth (John 3:11; 14:6). He, with the Father, is the supreme ruler of all creation.

59. Really none at all. This is the only congregation of the seven in which Jesus seems to find nothing to praise.

60. The people were not only tepid in their Christianity; they were content to be so. Because of their material prosperity, they found their security in their possessions and wealth. They even boasted of their affluence.

61. Jesus called upon this church to turn to Him to find the gold to make them spiritually rich, white clothes to cover their spiritual nakedness, and eye salve to heal their spiritual blindness. Jesus suggested that He might have to discipline and rebuke them to move them to repent, but He would do it in love.

62. Christ offered to enter the hearts and lives of these people to bless them and to give them the right to sit with Him on the throne of glory.

63. Applications to life today should be easy to make.

Lesson 3

Lamb Enthroned in Heaven

Theme verse: *And they sang a new song: "You are worthy to take the scroll and to open its seals, because You were slain, and by Your blood You purchased men for God from every tribe and language and people and nation. You have made them to be a kingdom and priests to serve our God, and they will reign on the earth."*

Revelation 5:9–10

See Brighton, *Revelation*, pp. 107–149.

Objectives

By the power of the Holy Spirit working through God's Word, we will

- affirm the significance that the setting of Revelation 4–5 has for a proper understanding of the book of Revelation;
- describe the scene before the throne of God and the significance of the various persons, objects, events, and symbols found in this scene;
- identify similarities between the vision of John in Revelation 4 and visions of Isaiah and Ezekiel;
- compare the symbolic language used in Revelation 4 with that used in other portions of Scripture;
- describe the scroll and its significance;
- describe the significance of the Lamb;
- affirm a desire to worship the Lamb in a thoughtful, meaningful manner.

The inaugural vision before the throne of God in Revelation 4–5 sets the tone for the entire book. Several thoughts are to be accented.

148

- God on His throne rules all things. He controls everything for the welfare of the church so that it may accomplish the purposes for which God established it. He also blesses the Gospel wherever it is proclaimed. This is a source of comfort for us in times of trial and an encouragement to be faithful in sharing the Word.
- Christ, seated at the right hand of the Father, dominates the book of Revelation.
- In chapter 5 we see the ascension of Jesus as viewed from heaven and His coronation to rule all things with the Father.
- The foundation of all of Revelation is the sacrificial, saving life, suffering, death, and resurrection of Jesus Christ.
- The heart of all of Revelation is the exalted reign of Christ. The prophecies of Revelation per se begin with chapter 6.

Before the Throne of God

Before the session, read Revelation 4 and thoroughly digest the material given in this section of the study guide so that you will be able to lead the presentation and discussion fluently. Because of the nature of the material, most of this section is expository.

64–66. Read and discuss these questions in the study guide.

67. Discuss the similarities between John's vision and the visions of Isaiah and Ezekiel.

a. Revelation 4:3/Ezekiel 1:28—In both cases a rainbow encircles God and His throne.

b. Revelation 4:5/Ezekiel 1:13—In both cases lightning is present.

c. Revelation 4:6/Ezekiel 1:5—In both cases four living creatures are present.

d. Revelation 4:7/Ezekiel 1:10—In Ezekiel each creature has four faces: that of a man, a lion, an ox, and an eagle. In Revelation one creature is like a lion, one is like an ox, one has the face of a man, and the fourth flies like an eagle.

e. Revelation 4:8/Ezekiel 1:18; 10:12—In both cases the living creatures are equipped with many eyes. In Revelation the creatures are covered with eyes. In Ezekiel each creature is associated with a wheel, the rim of which is full of eyes.

f. Revelation 4:8/Isaiah 6:2—In both cases the creatures have six wings. Those in Ezekiel's vision have four (Ezekiel 1:11). In Isaiah the creatures are seraphim (seraphs), while those in Ezekiel are cherubim.

An Unending Hymn of Praise

Read and discuss this section.

68. The triple holy indicates the infinite holiness of God. You might suggest to students that they read through the hymn "Holy, Holy, Holy" (*LW* 168, *TLH* 246), noting the ways the words of the hymn echo the thoughts of this chapter of Revelation.

69. The elders praise God for creating all things by His will.

70. The God who gave us life sent His Son to offer us new life through Him. Our redemption was something only God could accomplish.

The Bible in Revelation

71. If time will allow, lead the students in a comparison of at least three of the sets of passages. One purpose is to lead students to an understanding of the unity and interrelatedness of all parts of the Bible—the Old Testament as well as the New. What John saw by revelation is the fulfillment of the promises in the Old Testament as well as in the New. If time is short, commend this section to the participant's personal study this week.

Who Is Worthy to Open the Scroll?

Read the material in this section. Encourage students to look up the Old Testament references.

"Worthy Is the Lamb"

72. The Lamb looked to have been slain. As a sacrificial lamb, Jesus willingly laid down His life to pay for our transgressions.

73. Jesus has complete might and is in full control of the affairs of people.

74. The seven eyes represent the seven spirits (the Holy Spirit) sent out into the earth. Through the Holy Spirit, Jesus sees all things. One might see in this a reference to the Holy Spirit's role as being sent

into the world to bring people to saving faith and to sustain believers in that faith.

75. Jesus was slain and with His blood He purchased people for God from every tribe, language, people, and nation. He made all these people whom He purchased to be a kingdom and priests to serve God. And He enabled these people not only to serve God, but to reign with Him forever in the new earth.

76. The angels praise the Lamb by saying that He is worthy to receive seven things: power, wealth, wisdom, strength, honor, glory, and praise.

77. This material about the angels is interesting. Because angels are confirmed in their eternal bliss, we tend to think of them as superior to human beings. But in the order of God's creation, human beings are at the apex. The angels' function is to serve human beings as well as God. They are deeply interested in human beings and the salvation that Jesus gained for them. 1 Peter 1:10–12; Luke 15:10; and Hebrews 1:14 describe aspects of this concern and the service of the angels for the welfare of human beings. So it is not strange that also in heaven they praise Jesus for the salvation and life He gained for humankind (Revelation 5:11–12).

78. Human sin affects all creation (e.g., contemporary environmental problems). The redemption accomplished by Jesus Christ will bring restoration and renewal not only to the human family, but also to the entire created universe. See Colossians 1:20 and Romans 8:18–22.

79. The praise of all creatures is directed to God the Father (who sits on the throne) and to Jesus, the Lamb. That Jesus receives the same praise as the Father emphasizes His divine nature.

For Reflection

80–81. These questions are designed to help participants internalize and apply the truths of the lesson to their personal lives.

Lesson 4

First Vision: Seven Seals

Theme verse: *For the Lamb at the center of the throne will be their shepherd; He will lead them to springs of living water. And God will wipe away every tear from their eyes.*

Revelation 7:17

See Brighton, *Revelation*, pp. 150–209.

Objectives

By the power of the Holy Spirit working through God's Word, we will

- describe the cyclical character of the revelation given to John;
- identify the meaning of each of the four horsemen;
- give one answer as to why the righteous often suffer while the wicked prosper;
- explain the significance of upheavals in nature and society in view of the Last Day;
- state what the meaning of the sealing of the 144,000 means for their personal lives;
- describe their blessedness and hope as they anticipate the Last Day.

The material in this section is basic for understanding the revelation of this book.

The Four Horsemen

Review the historical background of Revelation as given in the Leader Notes. Throughout the early centuries pagans often blamed

Christians for the problems of the world. They believed that the ancient gods were offended by the spread of Christianity, and were punishing humankind for deserting them. It was in defense of Christianity against this kind of accusation that St. Augustine wrote *The City of God* (written between A.D. 413 and 426).

82. The red horse and its rider symbolize war and bloodshed. No particular war is meant; every war and rumor of war from the time of Jesus until the end is included.

83. The black horse and its rider depict famine and economic imbalance.

84. The pale horse represents disease and death.

Point out that all of the things pictured will affect the world until its end.

85. Accept students' responses from history and the world today of situations created by each of the four horsemen.

86. Point out that the things are the result of sin in the world. God desires to give people salvation and to bless them with His good gifts regardless of their external circumstances.

The Fifth Seal

87. The first thing to note is the souls whom John sees under the altar of the heavenly tabernacle. They are believers who have died but are awaiting the final judgment. This supports the view that after death believers do not "cease to exist" nor "enter a state of sleep" until the judgment but are in a state of bliss between the time of death and resurrection. They do not fear the final judgment but long for it. While on earth, these saints were persecuted for their adherence to the Word of God, yet they remained steadfast to the testimony of Jesus. This is most likely a reference to all believers who have died, those who experienced martyrdom, as well as those who were persecuted and tempted to renounce their faith in more subtle ways and yet were faithful.

88. These souls are crying to be vindicated not out of spirit of vengeance, but because they know firsthand the pain caused by evil, and they long to see the triumph of God and His truth and justice. They long for evil to be punished and done away with forever. Their address to God acknowledges His power, holiness, and genuineness. They know that His truth will triumph; they just long for it to be soon.

89. In response to this plea each saint is given the personal robe of righteousness gained by Jesus Christ—the assurance that they are truly members of the great family of God. It is because they are clothed with Jesus' righteousness that they have no fear of the final judgment. Jesus bore their judgment for them.

They are reminded that the end will not come until their number is complete; that is, through the death of the martyrs God wins His victory over the powers of evil, and only complete, total victory will bring about the consummation of God's purpose.

The Great Earthquake

90. Have students look up the passages listed and note the descriptions of the end of the world. Allusions to these passages in this section of Revelation are obvious. Note the following points:

a. God will destroy all that proud and arrogant people have lifted up in idolatry (Isaiah 2:12–22).

b. There will be no escaping the punishment of the Lord (Isaiah 24:1–23).

c. In His wrath God will destroy the creation (Isaiah 34:2–4).

You may want to extend the discussion to the false idealism of those who believe that human beings can create a perfect society. Such efforts can be temporarily helpful, but ultimately they are futile. This world and all therein is passing away.

91. Note that Jesus lists wars (Luke 21:9–10) and earthquakes, famines, and pestilences (21:11) as preludes to the end. Jesus is describing the same things John saw in his vision of the horsemen. Then Jesus talks about persecution (21:12). The souls that John saw under the altar had been persecuted. Be sure to note that all of these things will take place at various times until the end of the world. In Luke 21:25–26, Jesus describes a scene very much like John saw when the sixth seal was opened. This will happen at the very end of this era.

92. When the great upheavals in nature happen, Jesus will appear on a cloud with power and great glory and will send His angels to gather all of the elect.

93. The people of God are to be careful not to be weighed down by the temptations or cares of this world. They are to watch and pray so that they may be found faithful in the day of the coming of the Lord and thus may escape the terrible judgment faced by unbelievers. They

will stand before Jesus and receive the acquittal He purchased for them with His blood.

The Sealing of the 144,000

Here we have the Christian church pictured as the New Israel—the chosen Israel of the New Testament era. Already in His ministry Jesus spoke of His disciples sitting "on twelve thrones, judging the twelve tribes of Israel" (Matthew 19:28; see also Luke 22:30). Paul wrote that the believer in Christ is the true Israelite, or Jew (Romans 2:29). He referred to the church as "the Israel of God" (Galatians 6:16). James addressed his letter to "the twelve tribes scattered among the nations" (James 1:1), and Peter used terminology from Isaiah 43:20 and Exodus 19:6 in referring to believers as "a chosen people, a royal priesthood, a holy nation" (1 Peter 2:9).

94. Encourage participants to look up the references in this section and to apply the passages to their lives. If time is short, read only two or three in class and commend the remaining passages to the participants for their own personal study this week.

The Song of Victory

Revelation 7:9–17 is one of the most familiar—and beautiful—sections of Revelation.

95. God's promise to Abraham was that his seed would be a great multitude that no one could number. The vision of heaven (Revelation 7:9) shows all of the spiritual seed of Abraham—"a great multitude that no one could count."

96. The palms point to the homage given Jesus already in Jerusalem on Palm Sunday. He is the promised Messiah in whom our sins have been cleansed (symbolized by the white robes) and through whose cleansing blood we now can appear before God.

97. Both Psalm 98 and Revelation 7:10, 12 are songs of praise to the Lord for the salvation He gives to all humankind.

98. We will serve God day and night in perfect happiness and bliss. We will never hunger, thirst, or experience pain or discomfort. God will wipe every tear from our eyes.

You might point out to students that Revelation 7:14 is more correctly translated as follows: "These are they who are coming out of the great tribulation." This depicts the saints of God coming out of the tribulation of the world when they die. It does not support the teaching that Christians will be raptured out of the great tribulation that precedes the end of the world.

Lesson 5

Second Vision: Seven Trumpets

Theme verse: *Another angel, who had a golden censer, came and stood at the altar. He was given much incense to offer, with the prayers of all the saints, on the golden altar before the throne. The smoke of the incense, together with the prayers of the saints, went up before God from the angel's hand.*

Revelation 8:3–4

See Brighton, *Revelation*, pp. 210–248.

Objectives

By the power of the Holy Spirit working through God's Word, we will
- describe the importance of prayer in the reign of Jesus until the Last Day;
- note the effects of sin on the physical world as indicated by the first four trumpet blasts;
- describe the growing warfare on humankind by Satan and his followers;
- describe the limitations that God places on Satan's assaults on humanity and the world;
- describe the rule of God's grace in a universe in which Satan and evil seem to be supreme.

Introduction

Because the cyclical structure of Revelation is so important for the proper understanding and interpretation of this book, use this introduction to review the nature and significance of the cycles.

Preparation for the Second Cycle

99. As Jesus rules during this period until the Last Day, He responds in His grace and wisdom to the prayers of His people on earth. As we live in a world filled with the woes of God's judgment, we have been sealed so that we might be safe, and we can commune with our Lord through prayer in the midst of the trials and tribulations that befall this world.

100. In Joel the trumpet announces the approach of the day of the Lord (the Last Day), a terrible day for unrepentant sinners. But until that day arrives people can still repent and return to the Lord who is gracious and merciful.

Nature Polluted

101. In Romans 8:19–22 Paul indicates that the entire physical universe suffers from the consequences of human sin. However, all of nature will be renewed when Jesus comes again to usher in the new heaven and the new earth.

102. Discuss student responses.

103. Catastrophic events in nature are signs of the end of this age. People can turn to the Lord for salvation. Those who call on His name will be saved.

104. That only a fraction is destroyed with each plague indicates that this punishment is not yet complete and final. The purpose of these visitations is to warn people of the wrath and judgment of God and to bring them to repentance and saving faith. In His grace and mercy God is patient.

105. The people of God have nothing to fear from these catastrophic events because God is their refuge and the one who gives them strength. He controls such events, and nothing can take them away from Him.

106. The first set of passages uses darkness as a symbol of divine judgment. In Colossians 1:13 Paul uses darkness to symbolize the rule of sin and Satan to which people are enslaved apart from Christ.

107. Note the similarities between the plagues of Egypt and those preceding the Last Day.

a. Both include the plague of hail (Exodus 9:13–35/Revelation 8:7).

b. Both include the turning of water into blood (Exodus 7:14–24/Revelation 8:8–9).

c. Both include darkness (Exodus 10:21–29/Revelation 8:12).

108. The Egyptian plagues preceded the exodus of God's people from the tyranny of Egypt to the Promised Land of Canaan. The plagues of Revelation precede the new exodus of God's people from the tyranny of this sinful world to the Promised Land of the age to come.

The Assault from the Abyss (The First Woe)

Discuss the material in this section.

The Reserves Are Brought In (The Second Woe)

109. By God's grace the church continues to teach the Word and administer the Sacraments unhindered in many parts of the world. The church continues to grow even in those places where those who follow Christ are most severely persecuted.

110. We are part of the church. It is our privilege and obligation to reach out to others with the saving Gospel as God opens doors for us and empowers us. Ask students for examples of how God has used them to share the Good News with someone else.

Lesson 6

Scenes in the Interlude

Theme verse: *"And I will give power to My two witnesses, and they will prophesy for 1,260 days, clothed in sackcloth." These are the two olive trees and the two lampstands that stand before the Lord of the earth.*

Revelation 11:3–4

See Brighton, *Revelation*, pp. 249–316.

Objectives

By the power of the Holy Spirit working through God's Word, we will
- describe at least two purposes for which God has left them in this world filled with so much evil;
- identify the Mighty One who has called them into mission;
- point out why they can fulfill their mission in confidence;
- understand why they can anticipate opposition and hostility as they seek to fulfill their God-given mission;
- explain why they can look toward the future, especially the end of their lives and of this world, with eager anticipation and joy.

Introduction

In the vision of the seven trumpets, John sees that which is to occur in church and society between the Lord's earthly ministry and the Last Day. Throughout the entire New Testament era God's people can expect to endure along with the world the results of sin in the form of calamities and death (although they are spared some of the suffering caused by the minions of Satan). In addition to general suffering, Christians can expect to suffer just because they are Christians. Here

160

John prepares the people of God for the tribulations to come and gives them the assurance that the living Jesus will be with them to sustain and support them and finally receive them into eternal bliss with Him at the throne of heaven.

The One Who Calls Us

111. Twice before John had seen Jesus with His face like the sun, once earlier in Revelation and before that at the transfiguration.

112. The rainbow might point to God's covenant of gracious forbearance with the people of the earth.

113. The cloud and fiery pillars would remind John's readers of the pillar of cloud and pillar of fire by which God led the Israelites during the exodus and in the wilderness. So God continues to lead His people as they travel the road of the exodus from the evil of this age to the eternal holiness and glory of heaven.

114. In these passages, clouds symbolize the judgment of God on humankind as well as His majesty.

115. The appearance of this angel suggests that it was probably Jesus Himself. If not, it was an angel closely associated with Him for the fulfilling of His will. Note that in the Old Testament when God appeared in human form, He was often called "the Angel of the Lord" (e.g., Judges 6:11–24).

116. By placing His right foot on the sea and His left foot on the land, the angel indicates God's control over the whole world. As we will see in the following section, John is commissioned to carry God's message to many peoples. The posture of the angel here may be further indication that God's message is for the entire world. It must be heard by all, for this message of God will dominate all history. This is why God has placed us also in the world today. God has called us for this mission, even as he called John in Revelation.

The Purpose and Task for Which We Are Called

117. Ezekiel is commissioned to speak God's Word to the house of Israel. John's mission is to proclaim God's Word before many peoples, nations, languages, and kings.

118. This commission is essentially that which Jesus gave all His disciples. While we do not receive direct revelation as did Ezekiel and John, we, like they, are called to proclaim God's Word.

119. Eating the scroll symbolizes reading and internalizing its message. We receive the Word, take it to heart, and then proclaim it.

120. That the scroll was sweet indicates joy in the promises of God. The Gospel of Jesus Christ itself is sweet and glorious. But the scroll also contains a word of judgment; its proclamation is often followed by bitter persecution and rejection.

121. We are to proclaim the Word of God to all people before the end of this age after which it will be too late for people to repent.

122. The Gospel of the kingdom will be preached to all nations before the end will come.

123. Give participants time to verbalize how they today might fulfill their vocation in this world as Christians, confessing Christ's name.

Confidence to Confess Boldly

Lead the students in a discussion of the material in this section. Take time to look up at least some of the Bible references listed. You may want to just skim the passages from Ezekiel and Zechariah.

The Church's Final Persecution and Triumph

124. The persecution will take place when the witnesses have finished their testimony. Recall Jesus' words and the similar vocabulary He used when He said that the Gospel must be preached in the entire world as a testimony to all nations and then the end would come (Matthew 24:14).

125. Revelation 11:7 is probably relating the same thing as Revelation 20:3, in which case this beast is Satan, who comes up from the abyss where he has been held for the entire Gospel era until this time. Note that although Satan was bound, he was not powerless. He is ultimately the source of all the persecutions that have plagued the church throughout its history. Now he has been released for one final and direct onslaught.

126. The phrase "will attack them" in Revelation 11:7 is more literally translated "will make war against them." This indicates that

the church is a sizable enemy, but Satan overpowers and kills it. This does not necessarily mean that all believers living on earth are physically killed but that the church as a definable, witnessing community is destroyed. The church is dead and ineffectual.

127. Sodom symbolizes immorality and great sin. Egypt symbolizes rebellion against God and oppression of His people. Together with the reference to Jerusalem, these symbolize not one specific place but the world in opposition to God.

128. Refusing to bury someone is a sign of great contempt. Note that those gazing on the bodies of the witnesses come from the world over. Whereas past persecutions of the church were often localized, this persecution results in the worldwide death of the church.

129. Unbelievers break out in celebration over the death of the church because they were tormented by the church's message of repentance and forgiveness which called them to renounce their sins, their heresies, and their seeming control over their own lives. With the church dead they figure they can live as they please with no one to challenge them.

130. After a short period of time, the breath of God restores the church. This recalls Ezekiel's vision in which breath from God made dead bones live, symbolizing God's restoration of His people.

131. Those who witness the church's return to life are terrified because this vindicates the church's message and points to their condemnation.

The Day of Triumph

The seventh trumpet sounds. For unbelievers this is the sound of judgment and eternal torment and death. Justice is served.

But for the people of God who placed their trust for life and salvation not in themselves and their works, but in the saving life and work of Jesus Christ, the blast of the seventh trumpet announces the beginning of eternal glory. This is a fine positive note on which to end the session.

Lesson 7

Woman With Child and the Dragon

Theme verse: *Then I heard a loud voice in heaven say: "Now have come the salvation and the power and the kingdom of our God, and the authority of His Christ. For the accuser of our brothers, who accuses them before our God day and night, has been hurled down.*

Revelation 12:10

See Brighton, *Revelation*, pp. 317–341.

Objectives

By the power of the Holy Spirit working through God's Word, we will
- identify the causes behind the outward struggle between the church and the world;
- explain the symbolism and meaning of the vision of the dragon, woman, and child;
- describe the significance of the war in heaven;
- express joy and confidence in the midst of opposition and hostility.

Introduction

Use the introductory material in the study guide to lay a foundation for the day's lesson.

Dragon, Woman, and Child

132. *Sign*—a great spectacle that points to the consummation of all earthly things. Jesus has told us that the Last Day will be preceded

164

by the following: "great earthquakes, famines and pestilences in various places, and fearful events and great signs from heaven" (Luke 21:11); "signs in the sun, moon and stars"; nations in "anguish and perplexity at the roaring and tossing of the sea" (Luke 21:25); "wonders in the heaven above and signs on the earth below, blood and fire and billows of smoke" (Acts 2:19).

133. The woman first represents the Old Testament people of God because it was from Israel that Christ came. After the child is born, the woman represents the church, the believers of the New Testament era.

134. Although despised by the world, from God's point of view His people are radiant, glorious, and exalted. And He has allowed them to share His reign.

135. This male child will defeat Satan (Genesis 3:15), will be God with us (Isaiah 7:14), will be called "Wonderful Counselor, Mighty God, Everlasting Father, Prince of Peace" (Isaiah 9:6). He will reign with power and might (Psalm 2:9), and He is the Son of God, "born of a woman, born under law, to redeem those under law, that we might receive the full rights of sons" (Galatians 4:4–5).

136. The dragon is Satan.

137. Not content with being creatures of God, certain angels wanted to be gods. They rebelled against Him to establish their own independence.

a. When these angels sinned, God condemned them to hell (2 Peter 2:4).

b. These forces of evil continue to battle against the people of God (Ephesians 6:12).

c. God has kept the angels who rebelled against Him in darkness, "bound with everlasting chains for judgment on the great Day" (Jude 6).

d. Our enemy, the devil, has always been and will always continue to be a murderer and a liar (John 8:44).

e. Sinners are the servants of the devil, but Jesus came to destroy the work of the devil (1 John 3:8).

138. The desert would have reminded John's readers of the desert in which the children of Israel lived for 40 years on their way to the Promised Land (Exodus 16:1–10). There, God fed them with food from heaven and provided that their clothes did not wear out and their feet

did not swell (Deuteronomy 8:2–5). Also, God provided for Elijah as he stayed by the brook in the Kerith Ravine through ravens who brought Elijah bread and meat (1 Kings 17:2–6). Another time when Elijah fled into the desert in order to escape Jezebel, God sent His angel to strengthen him (1 Kings 19:2–9).

Perhaps John's reader were also reminded of the flight of Mary, Joseph, and the baby Jesus to Egypt (Matthew 2:13–15) or of Hosea's leading his wife into the desert to comfort and encourage her (Hosea 2:14–15).

139. Through the Word of God we have the saving knowledge of all that God in Christ has done for us. Plus we enjoy the fellowship of others who trust in Jesus and of the fellowship of the Father, and Christ as well as others (1 John 1:3). We also enjoy grace and peace of our Lord, the love of God, and the fellowship of the Holy Spirit (2 Corinthians 13:11–14).

140. Answers will vary.

War in Heaven

141. An example of Satan accusing the people of God can be found in the account of Job (Job 1:6–12). Satan stated that Job worshiped God only because of the material rewards he had received in return for his devotion. Zechariah 3:1 pictures Satan before God accusing Israel's High Priest at the time, namely Joshua, of having fallen short of God's standards. Joshua was able to stand because the Lord had taken away his sin (3:4–5), not because of his personal piety or perfection.

142. Revelation 12:10–12 is a beautiful description of the victory over Satan and his accusations and the sure hope of eternal life with God won for us by Jesus through His life, death, and resurrection.

143. This hymn also includes a most solemn warning to those on earth against the determined efforts of Satan to destroy them.

144. In Romans 8, Paul also confesses unequivocally that Satan cannot rightly bring any charge or condemnation against God's people because Christians are secure in the protecting grace of God. Furthermore, Satan cannot separate Christians from God's love.

War on Earth

145. Even as God delivered His people from the tyranny of the Egyptians by carrying them on eagles' wings, so He gives the church eagles' wings to flee the tyranny of the devil. This symbolizes God's care for and protection of His people.

146. Satan will not only pursue the church as a whole but will make war on individual believers (her offspring).

147. God's people overcome Satan by the blood of Jesus, shed for their forgiveness, and the word of their testimony, that is, the Gospel which they share with others while here on earth. Note that they are even willing to give up their physical life in the struggle knowing that they will live forever with the Lord.

148. Summarize the session by giving students opportunity to identify some of the problems they might expect because of their allegiance to Christ, but also the joy and confidence they have in God.

Lesson 8

Two Beasts and the Conquering Lamb

Theme verse: *Then I looked, there before me was the Lamb, standing on Mount Zion, and with Him 144,000 who had His name and His Father's name written on their foreheads.*

Revelation 14:1

See Brighton, *Revelation*, pp. 342–394.

Objectives

By the power of the Holy Spirit working through God's Word, we will
- describe how Satan uses tyrannical political powers to accomplish his deceptive and destructive goals;
- describe how anti-Christian philosophies and religions seek the destruction of human souls;
- describe the mission of the three angels;
- describe the warning and the reassurance they receive from this lesson;
- praise God for His power and grace that enables them to live victoriously.

The Beast from the Sea

Revelation 13 shows us the instruments that the dragon (Satan) uses for his attack on the people of God.

149. Similarities between Daniel 7:1–28 and Revelation 13:1–10 are, among others, the following items:

a. Daniel saw four great beasts arise from the sea (Daniel 7:3). The beast of Revelation also emerged from the sea (13:1).

b. One of the four beasts of Daniel was like a lion, one like a bear, and one like a leopard (7:4–6). In Revelation, "the beast [John] saw resembled a leopard, but had feet like those of a bear and a mouth like that of a lion" (13:2).

c. The fourth beast of Daniel (7:7) had ten horns. The beast of Revelation also had ten horns (13:1).

Other similarities can be noted. Note the identification in Daniel of these beasts as political powers (7:17).

150. The imagery of Revelation 13 also appears elsewhere in the Bible as follows:

a. In both Revelation 13:1 and Isaiah 17:12 the sea represents the violent character of nations and political forces.

b. The leopard represents swiftness, cunning; it is large and fierce, swift to spring on its prey.

c. A bear is ready to rend and tear, eager with its great and terrible feet to crush the enemy.

d. The growling and roaring lion, eager to have its prey, is anxious to destroy.

151. The beast was given power to make war against God's people and conquer them.

152. Some examples of tyrannical powers in biblical times are Egypt, Assyria, Babylon, the Greece of Alexander the Great, Syria, and Rome. Located at the crossroads of the ancient world, Palestine was always vulnerable to the marching armies of the great powers. John was most likely thinking of Rome.

153. One notable example would be the former Soviet Union. It is interesting that in the Soviet Union (and in China today) the church continued in spite of intense persecution. It went into hiding, to be sure, but it emerged perhaps stronger than ever.

154. Answers will vary.

155. One purpose is to bring people to repentance and faith. God's people may wander from Him. God permits affliction to happen in order to bring them back.

156. The passages cited are clear; the questions are designed for open discussion. Note that Christians are obliged to obey civil

authority. But when commands of the civil authority cannot be obeyed without sin, we "must obey God rather than men" (Acts 5:29).

157. To worship this beast would mean to place one's trust for one's highest good in the political, economic, and social institutions of this world rather than in God.

158. As we have seen before in Revelation, the phrase "all inhabitants of the earth" refers to unbelievers. This verse makes that clear beyond a doubt by noting that those who worship the beast are those whose names are not written in the Lamb's book of life. By inference, those whose names are written there (believers) do not worship the beast.

159. The passages cited are clear; the questions are designed for open discussion.

The Beast out of the Earth

160. That the beast has two horns like a lamb might indicate that this beast appears to be like Christ. At the least, the appearance of this beast is that of a meek creature.

161. The voice of the beast, which is like that of a dragon, gives the beast away. In truth, the beast is ferocious and destructive like the dragon—Satan.

162. Jesus warns us to watch out for false teachers. Although they are ferocious wolves (ready to devour their prey), they appear as meek and harmless as sheep. But they can be recognized for who they are by the products of their teaching.

163. This beast is antithetical to the Holy Spirit. The Holy Spirit leads people to confess and believe, "Jesus is Lord" (1 Corinthians 12:3). Although false teachers do not always serve political authority (as the cult of emperor worship supported Rome in John's day), many times they do. In all cases they lead people away from trust in God to trust in human power, human philosophy, or human institutions.

164. The second beast deceives with "great and miraculous signs" (Revelation 13:13). Jesus tells us in Matthew 24:23–24 that false Christs and false prophets will deceive people with "great signs and miracles."

165. The beast will only be able to deceive the inhabitants of the earth, that is, the unbelievers. Note that in Matthew 24:24, Jesus

indicates that these false prophets would deceive even the elect, but that is not possible.

166. The consequence of refusing to worship the image of the first beast is death. Not having the mark of the beast makes it impossible for believers to trade, meaning that they would not be able to function in that economic system, even to buy food. Christians should not be surprised if their loyalty to Christ leads them to economic ruin or even to death.

The Triumph of the Saints

167. We have encountered the number 144,000 before in Revelation (7:4). Here as there it stands for all the people of God from Adam and Eve down to those believers living at the Last Day. (The 144,000 equals the Old Testament believers represented by the 12 tribes of Israel times the New Testament believers represented by the 12 apostles times 1,000, the number that indicates ultimate perfection and completeness.) Not one of God's chosen people, regularly nourished by the Spirit through the Word, will be lost to Satan.

168. Jesus' name and the Father's name are written on the foreheads of the saints; that is, they belong to God and the Lamb.

169. These saints are virgins, that is, by the power of the Spirit they persevered in their faithfulness to Christ.

The Mission of the Angels

170. Luke 17:26–30 suggests that many people are lost because in this life they are so preoccupied with everyday activities that they ignore God and their eternal welfare.

171. Examples of indifference to warnings of judgment and the Gospel include materialism, disrespect for God's Word and the holy ministry, declines in church membership, preoccupation with self-satisfaction. Poor Bible study habits, "Sunday" Christianity, lack of zeal for mission work, and poor stewardship all indicate complacency on the part of the people of God. This spirit can be overcome only by the power of the Spirit of God, who works in human hearts through the Word and the Sacraments.

172. Answers will include times students can reach out with the Word of God especially to those who in their absorption with the

challenges and charms of this world are unconcerned and indifferent about their future and eternal well-being.

173. It is difficult to endure patiently, obey God's commandments, and remain faithful to Jesus because the temptations around us are so great. Opinion may vary as to whether it is more difficult today to persevere than in former ages. End this discussion on a note of assurance that God who is faithful gives His people the strength to persevere in faith.

The Final Harvest

174. In this age God permits the weeds (unbelievers) to grow with the grain (believers). However, at the end of this world in His divine and final judgment God will separate the weeds from the grain. Both Revelation 14:14–20 and Matthew 13:24–30 tell of this.

175. Both Daniel 7:13–14 and Revelation 14:14 speak of Jesus as the Son of Man, a term Jesus preferred using when referring to Himself. In both passages the Son of Man comes on the clouds of heaven to judge and to receive universal and lasting dominion. The crown points to Him as the Messiah who has conquered and thereby earned the right to act in judgment. The sharp sickle is the instrument of harvest and depicts the Son of Man as coming to harvest the earth in judgment.

176. Give students an opportunity to respond to this question if they would like to do so.

Lesson 9

Third Vision: Seven Censers

Theme verse: *And [they sing] the song of Moses, the servant of God and the song of the Lamb: "Great and marvelous are Your deeds, Lord God Almighty! Just and true are Your ways, King of the ages. Who will not fear You, O Lord, and bring glory to your name? For You alone are holy. All nations will come and worship before You, for Your righteous acts have been revealed."*

Revelation 15:3–4

See Brighton, *Revelation*, pp. 395–430.

Objectives

By the power of the Holy Spirit working through God's Word, we will

- explain why Christians can rejoice in the midst of those tribulations that God permits to befall the world as the consequences of human sin;
- describe the glorious state of the saints in heaven;
- tell how God uses disorders in nature to punish the enemies of His people;
- recognize how God also uses political unrest for judgment on those who oppose Him and oppress His people;
- identify the message of hope all Christians have while living in the midst of a decaying world.

It is good to review once again the cyclical structure of Revelation as an introduction to the third vision. Each vision depicts events that occur from the time of Christ to His second coming, events that point to the end. Each vision ends with a view of Judgment Day.

173

However, each vision approaches this from a somewhat different perspective. This third and final vision emphasizes the final judgments to be poured out on humankind.

The Church Triumphant

177. The previous sign was the woman symbolizing God's people. The whole history of the church has been one of conflict between the offspring of the woman (the Savior, Genesis 3:15) and Satan and his followers. The sign of Revelation 15 reveals God's judgments on the oppressors of His people. These plagues belong to the drama of the continuing conflict between the church and the world led by Satan.

178. The sea of Revelation 15:2 may allude to the Red Sea through which the exodus from Egypt occurred. Following the exodus, the people of Israel watched as the sea was used by God to defeat their enemies. In Revelation we see standing next to this fiery sea, those who have come out of this world and who will now witness the judgment of God against their enemies.

179. This description of all believers who endure faithfully in spite of persecution refers back to chapter 13. These are those who did not worship the beast and his image and who did not receive his mark.

180. The song of Moses in Exodus 15 celebrated the deliverance of the Israelites at the Red Sea, while the song of Moses and the Lamb in Revelation 15 celebrates the deliverance of humanity through the sacrificial life, suffering, death, and resurrection of Jesus Christ. Both songs praise God for His mighty deeds of salvation and His majesty.

181. After the exodus, God instructed Moses to build the tabernacle as His dwelling place among the Israelites (Exodus 25:8–9). During the travels of the Israelites in the desert, God dwelt within the tabernacle with its ark of the covenant (Exodus 40:34–35). Within this ark were kept the two tablets of the Law that Moses received on Mount Sinai (Deuteronomy 10:5). These tablets were called the "two tablets of the Testimony" (Exodus 32:15), hence the name of the tabernacle used in Revelation 15:5. Here we see the heavenly tabernacle, after which the earthly tabernacle was patterned. The use of this figure points out that the seven censers are God's judgment on the unbelieving world.

182. Frequently throughout the Old Testament, clouds and smoke indicated God's presence and His glory. This visible sign of God's presence among His people appeared in the tabernacle and then in the temple. The holiness and majesty of the divine presence were so overwhelming that sinful humans were often not able to be in the same room.

183. The gold indicates the censers are to be used for God's purposes. The censers are full to indicate the fierceness and unmitigated character of God's wrath. It is everlasting wrath for it proceeds from the eternal God. This judgment is final and one that will endure throughout eternity.

Plagues of Nature

Unless students wish to review the plagues of Egypt, it is not necessary to read the Exodus passage. As a class you might compare the seven trumpets with the seven censers.

There are close parallels between these two visions, but whereas the first four plagues of the trumpet vision affect only part of the world, the plagues of the first four censers affect the entire world. This fits with the emphasis on "last plagues" in Revelation 15:1.

184. Physical health, salt water, fresh water, and the sun are affected by the first four plagues.

185. Both Revelation 16:1–9 and Matthew 24:29–31 emphasize that catastrophes in the physical universe will be a sign that this age is passing away and that the Lord will return to make all things new.

186. The first plague hits those who bear the mark of the beast and worship his image (Revelation 13:15–17).

187. The third plague—which turns fresh water to blood—is a fitting judgment on the enemies of God who spilled the blood of saints and prophets.

188. Although these plagues are judgments of God on His enemies, until the final judgment, God's judgments also serve the purpose of leading people to repentance. However, we are again cautioned about expecting many to repent.

189. This question is for application to personal life. Students might emphasize remaining faithful to escape the judgment of God and being diligent witnesses in order that others too might escape by

trusting in the only means of escape—Jesus, who bore God's judgment for us.

Plagues among the Nations

Read and discuss this section with class participants.

The End of All Things

190. Discuss the similarities between the visions.

a. Great voices in heaven proclaim the realization of the kingdom of God (11:15); a great voice from the heavenly throne declares that God's purpose has been accomplished (16:17).

b. In Revelation 11:19 we read that the heavenly temple of God is opened, and there are flashes of lightning, rumblings, peals of thunder, an earthquake, and a great hailstorm; in Revelation 16:18, 21 we read that there are flashes of lightning, rumblings, peals of thunder, the greatest of all earthquakes, and tremendous hail.

191. The cup of God's wrath is symbolic of God's judgment. Babylon the Great, symbolizing all the enemies of God's people, must drink that cup, that is, they must receive God's judgment. Jesus drank the cup of God's wrath for us. Students will likely be able to answer this last question without looking up the Matthew passage; however, they should read it in this context. It is quite possible that Jesus was referring to the cup of God's wrath in the Garden of Gethsemane.

192. In spite of all the evidences of God's judgment on sin, many unbelievers persist in their unbelief and evil ways.

193. In Revelation 16:9, repentance is mentioned, so it must still be possible, even though unlikely. It is possible because the final judgment has not yet come. In 16:21, repentance is not mentioned—likely because it is no longer possible. The final judgment has come.

194. The curses of unbelievers indicate that they blame God for the judgments that befall them; they do not acknowledge that their sin brought the judgments. The believers on the other hand praise God for being just and true, and thereby acknowledge that those who receive judgment do indeed deserve it. The marvelous deeds for which the believers praise God include their redemption from sin through Jesus

176

and the judgment that they, too, would have had to bear had not Christ bore it for them.

195. A discussion question for personal application.

Lesson 10

Fall of Babylon

Theme Verse: *Rejoice over her, O heaven! Rejoice, saints and apostles and prophets! God has judged her for the way she treated you.*

Revelation 18:20

See Brighton, *Revelation*, pp. 431–483.

Objectives

By the power of the Holy Spirit working through God's Word, we will

- identify the allurements of the great prostitute of Revelation 17–18;
- flee her influence;
- realize that our faithfulness to Christ may entail losing our lives;
- recognize the control of God over all earthly events;
- rejoice in the destruction that will befall the great enemies of God.

The Prostitute and the Beast

This paragraph and material on Babylon provides background on the imagery of Babylon. You will probably want to have participants skim the longer Old Testament passages rather than read them in their entirety. Or commend the passages to the students for personal study outside class.

196. Babylon is called a prostitute because she not only commits adultery, she entices others into adultery.

197. Adultery is a common Old Testament metaphor for idolatry and apostasy. God is the faithful husband, and His people the unfaithful wife, who prostitutes herself by worshiping idols and trusting in foreign powers rather than in God for her security.

198. The rulers of the earth and the inhabitants of the earth (unbelievers).

199. The inhabitants of the earth are drunk, that is, they are totally caught up in this adultery and they can't think clearly. In 18:23 Babylon's influence is described as a magic spell.

200. The attire of the prostitute exudes not only royalty (symbolized by the colors) but enormous wealth. And as we see from chapter 18, she shares that wealth with all who commit adultery with her.

201. The cup is filled with abominable and filthy things. The allurements of the world—in reality—offer nothing but filth.

202. The prostitute's title reveals that this is indeed Babylon the Great and that she is not only a prostitute, but that she brings forth other prostitutes and the abominations of the earth.

203. Babylon the Great not only sheds the blood of the saints (those who witness to Jesus), she revels in doing it and gets drunk on their blood.

204. The woman has influence throughout the world and will lead all nations astray.

205. This beast, the beast from the sea in chapter 13, symbolizes the civil governments of this world in their anti-Christian aspect.

206. Both Revelation 13 and Revelation 17 note the astonishment of the unbelievers.

207. According to Revelation 17:8 this astonishment is called forth by the fact that the beast "once was, now is not, and will come." This aspect of the beast is pictured in chapter 13 as the fatal wound that had healed. As in chapter 13, this symbolizes that when one anti-Christian government has fallen, another will rise in its place.

208. This description of the beast, along with his blasphemous names (17:3), indicates that this beast has placed himself in the position of God. The power and seeming invincibility of the beast draws forth the astonishment and allegiance of unbelievers. The beast comes from the abyss, which indicates his satanic origin.

209. This king, the beast himself, is going to his destruction.

210. The one purpose of these kings and the beast is to make war on the Lamb.

211. The Lamb will be victorious because He is "Lord of lords and King of kings" (17:14). He will be accompanied by His called, chosen, and faithful followers.

212. God accomplishes His purpose by letting the beast destroy the prostitute.

Babylon Has Fallen!

213. Although God's people must live in the world influenced by the prostitute, they are not to be taken in by her allurements. They are to separate themselves from her and refuse to share in her sins that they might not experience her judgment.

214. Babylon, great though she is, will fall in a very short period of time ("one day" in 18:8; "one hour" in 18:10).

215. They have lost their source of wealth and luxury, and they are terrified that her fate will befall them also.

216. Babylon will be completely and totally destroyed.

217. The reaction of the prophets, apostles, and saints of God (all God's people) is to be one of rejoicing because God has judged the great prostitute for shedding their blood.

Lesson 11

Song of Victory
and Second Coming

Theme verse: *Then the angel said to me, "Write: Blessed are those who are invited to the wedding supper of the Lamb." And he added, "These are the true words of God."*

Revelation 19:9

See Brighton, *Revelation*, pp. 484–532.

Objectives

By the power of the Holy Spirit working through God's Word, we will

- express joy in the future that they have in Jesus Christ;
- praise God for His victory over all evil forces that seek to destroy His people;
- explain how Christ's relationship with His people can be described as a marriage;
- describe and explain the significance of the vision of the rider on the white horse;
- express personal assurance derived from the visions reported in Revelation 19.

God's people praise God for His salvation, glory, and power and for justly condemning the great prostitute and thus avenging the blood of His saints which she spilled.

Marriage Feast of the Lamb

218. Reflect with your students on the following passages that use the bridegroom and bride imagery to tell of the relationship of the Lord and His people:

a. Isaiah 62:5—Here God is compared to a bridegroom who rejoices over His bride, the new Israel.

b. Jeremiah 2:31–32—Israel's unfaithfulness is compared to a bride who forgets her wedding ornaments.

c. 2 Corinthians 11:2—Here Paul writes of Christ as the husband and the church as the pure virgin.

d. Ephesians 5:25–32—The relationship between husband and wife is compared to that of Christ and His church.

e. Revelation 21:9–10—The Lamb is compared to the bridegroom whose wife is the church.

219. The fine linen represents the righteousness bestowed on the people of God through the sacrificial blood of the Lamb.

220. The phrase "*given* her to wear" (italics added) emphasizes that our righteousness and our salvation are free gifts bestowed on us by God for the sake of the sacrificial life, suffering, death, and resurrection of our Savior, Jesus Christ.

221. Angels are creatures of God who worship and serve God. They are not to be worshiped. Only God is worthy of worship.

The Victor Receives His Victory

222. The rider on the white horse is Christ, who is completely faithful and true. Therefore, we can fully and safely entrust to Him our whole being and future. The whiteness of the horse indicates the purity of our Lord, a purity He also bestows on all His followers. Also, Christ will judge in purity and righteousness all those who rejected His gracious offer of salvation and life.

223. Jesus comes to judge in righteousness and justice all those who in this lifetime rejected His grace, forgiveness, and life. A person can be judged either in justice or by God's grace in Christ. Those who choose justice will surely be condemned eternally because of their sin. But by the power and wisdom of the Holy Spirit, others are led to rely on the redemption purchased for them by Christ. They are assured of eternal life.

224. Christ will judge righteously and with omniscience.

225. The blood may be that of Christ's enemies, whom He has vanquished. It might also be a reference to the blood that Jesus shed on Calvary for our salvation.

226. Jesus is God's own Word revealed to humanity. To know Jesus is to know God.

227. The sword is the Word of God. The Law condemns us for our sin. If we persist in living under the Law, we will perish because no human being can fulfill it. The Gospel reveals to us our Savior, and through it the Holy Spirit implants saving faith within us, sustains us in that faith, empowers us for holy living, and leads us safely amid all the temptations and troubles of this life to our eternal home.

228. The quotation and the name indicate that Jesus has absolute authority that no one can resist. He is Lord of all.

229. Revelation 19:18 indicates the totality of the human enemies of God who will be defeated. None will be excluded.

230. Encourage participants to discuss the meaning of Revelation 19 for their personal lives of faith.

Lesson 12

Millennium and Judgment

Theme Verse: *And I saw the dead, great and small, standing before the throne, and books were opened. Another book was opened, which is the book of life. The dead were judged according to what they had done as recorded in the books.*

Revelation 20:12

See Brighton, *Revelation*, pp. 533–587.

Objectives

By the power of the Holy Spirit working through God's Word, we will

- describe the classical Christian understanding of Revelation 20;
- explain why believers can be confident of an eventual victory in spite of the growing opposition and hostility of Christ's enemies;
- identify the grace of God in Christ as being the foundation for their confidence of eternal salvation;
- describe briefly the various millennial theories and explain how they are contrary to Scripture.

The Millennium

231. All of these passages contain the promise that God's kingdom and the salvation He has provided will spread throughout the world.

232. The passages describe aspects of the conflict between Jesus and Satan that occurred during Jesus' earthly ministry.

a. Jesus resisted the devil's temptations (Matthew 4:1–11; Luke 4:1–13).

b. Jesus cast out demons, but He would not let the demons speak because they knew who He was. The teachers of the law accused Jesus of using the devil's power to cast out these evil forces, but Jesus pointed out that Satan's house would be divided and fall if he fought against himself. In His illustration of tying up the owner of the house before robbing that house, Jesus described what He was doing to Satan; Jesus was binding Satan so that He could rob him of his power (Mark 1:34; 3:20–30).

c. Jesus healed a man possessed by a legion of demons and cast the demons into a herd of swine (Mark 5:1–20).

d. One time the demon in a possessed man cried out identifying Jesus as the "Holy One of God." Jesus then cast the demon out of the man (Mark 1:21–28).

e. Though the prince of the world seemed to have triumphed with the death of Jesus on the cross, the death of Jesus was really the devil's defeat (John 12:30–33).

233. The second resurrection is the bodily resurrection that will occur on the Last Day when the souls of all who have died, both believers and unbelievers, will be reunited with their bodies.

234. The second death is eternal condemnation in hell.

Satan's Doom

Read and discuss this section.

The Great Judgment

Read and discuss this section.

235. The great comfort to be found in Revelation 20:14 is that death, which causes people such great suffering, will be destroyed forever.

Millennial Theories

236. In spite of our sin and unworthiness, our substitute, Jesus Christ, perfectly fulfilled God's Law on our behalf and endured the divine punishment for our sin. Therefore, we face Jesus' second

coming and Judgment Day with the assurance that we are the people of God and heirs of heaven.

237. God has placed us in this world to care for it, seek its peace, and, above all, live as children of light, witnesses to God's saving work in Jesus Christ.

238. Upon our physical death we are with the Lord.

239. Christ's second coming will occur at the end of this age. He will then raise all who have died. Believers will live forever with the Lord.

240. Christ's second coming will be sudden and unexpected; therefore all predictions of the time of His coming are futile. In fact, He has discouraged us from speculating by urging us to be ready at all times.

241. Rather than envisioning a millennium of peace and prosperity prior to the second coming, Scripture clearly and unequivocally affirms that evil and unbelief will abound in this world to the very end. The optimistic passages appealed to by millennialists foretell the spiritual glory of the New Testament church and the spread of the Gospel throughout the world.

242. Only one passage, 1 Thessalonians 4:13–17, speaks unequivocally of the rapture. In this passage Paul's point is that at the second coming those who are then living will not have an advantage over those "who have fallen asleep."

243. Romans 11:25–26 does not teach that all Jews will eventually be saved, even as it does not affirm the universal salvation of Gentiles. In Romans 9:6–8, Paul specifically states that all Israel is not made up of the physical descendants of Abraham, but of all those who, with Abraham, place their trust in the promises of God as centered in Jesus Christ.

Lesson 13

New Heaven and New Earth

Theme verse: *And I heard a loud voice from the throne saying, "Now the dwelling of God is with men, and He will live with them. They will be His people, and God Himself will be with them and be their God. He will wipe every tear from their eyes. There will be no more death or mourning or crying or pain, for the old order of things has passed away."*

Revelation 21:3–4

See Brighton, *Revelation*, pp. 588–660.

Objectives

By the power of the Holy Spirit working through God's Word, we will

- acknowledge that perfect peace, prosperity, and security will be established only in the world that is to come after the Last Day;
- describe the similarities between the first paradise (Genesis 1–2) and the paradise that is to come (Revelation 21–22);
- describe the new heaven and the new earth as depicted in Revelation 21;
- describe the new Jerusalem as portrayed in Revelation 21–22;
- express an understanding of how they are to prepare for the final consummation of this age.

244a. Genesis 1:1/Revelation 21:1—God created the heavens and the earth/God will establish a new heaven and a new earth.

b. Genesis 1:14–19/Revelation 21:23–25; 22:5—God created light/in the new heaven and earth there will be no need for created light because the glory of God gives it light and the Lamb is its lamp.

c. Genesis 3:1/Revelation 21:8—Satan is cunning and succeeds/Satan's work is destroyed.

d. Genesis 3:8/Revelation 21:3—Mankind is alienated from God and flees from Him/mankind is redeemed and lives in closest fellowship with God.

e. Genesis 3:16–19/Revelation 22:3—Humanity and the earth are cursed because of Adam and Eve's sin/there is no more curse.

f. Genesis 3:22/Revelation 22:14—Sinful people are forbidden to eat of the tree of life/those who have washed their robes in the blood of the Lamb now eat freely of the tree of life.

g. Genesis 3:22–24/Revelation 22:2—Paradise is lost/paradise is restored.

A New Heaven and a New Earth

245. This present universe is decaying and passing away. Note the different ways in which the cited passages describe this impermanence.

246. John sees the fulfillment of a promise made by God centuries before Christ through the prophet Isaiah and looked forward to by Peter.

247. "Coming down out of heaven from God" describes how God Himself takes the initiative to reestablish the close relationship that existed between Himself and humanity in the Garden of Eden. In the new heaven and earth this intimate relationship between God and His people will continue forever.

248. Just as the church is sometimes described as the new Israel, here the new Jerusalem symbolizes the church, the bride of the Lamb. John may also have in mind a literal city that God will build in the new earth, or this may be a completely figurative description of the holy Christian church.

249. Throughout the history of God's people, God used events and places and images and experiences to point forward to the new creation that would culminate that history. The passages point forward to the following aspects of the new creation:

a. God dwelling among His people.

b. God being their God and making them His people.

c. No more tears.

d. The end of death; no more tears or disgrace.

e. Joy and gladness forever; no more sorrow or sighing.

f. God's eternal presence with His people.

g. Those in Christ being made new.

h. God's people being His temple (His dwelling place) and God being their God and making them His people.

250. We experience this bliss most intimately in the Lord's Supper, which is a "foretaste of the feast to come" (*LW*, p. 169).

251. God promises to make our whole universe entirely new. We can count on it because His words are trustworthy and true. In this new heaven and earth, only perfect righteousness and peace will exist. This new universe is given to us to enjoy forever without price—it is the free gift of God's grace in Jesus Christ, our Savior, who is the water of life. The sin that condemns people to hell is to reject Jesus, the water of life.

The Holy City

Lead students in a discussion of this section.

Jesus Is Coming!

252. What was revealed to John is reality. We reject it to our own eternal destruction.

253. Jesus will return soon and suddenly, when we may least expect Him. In a real sense, He comes for each of us at the time of our physical death. Many people die with no advance warning. We are always to be prepared for Him when He comes to take us.

254. We are assured Jesus will come soon to take us into eternal blessedness.

255. All those who reject Christ and serve evil and Satan will be cast into eternal separation from God and everything that is good.

256. The Spirit of God and God's grace in Christ enable us to persevere in our relationship with God until Christ comes again to take us to be with Him forever.

Glossary

Amillennialism. The Biblical teaching (*a*-millennial means *no*-millennium) that the thousand years mentioned in Revelation 20:1–10 is symbolic for Christ's heavenly reign as King from the time of His ascension to His reappearing on the Last Day.

Antichrist. Based on 1 John 2:18, 22, 4:2–3 and 2 John 7, an *antichrist* is one who opposes the teachings of Christ or takes His place. The term is also used to describe "the lawless one" (2 Thessalonians 2:8) or the beast of the earth (Revelation 13:11–18), a deceptive religious leader or final Antichrist who emerges at the end of time.

Apocalyptic literature. (Greek: *apokalypsis*, or "revelation.") This type of literature, used especially in Revelation and Daniel, uses highly symbolic language in expressing theological truth.

Age of accountability. According to millennialists, infants and young children are not held accountable for their sins until they reach a certain level of maturity. Therefore they will be "raptured" along with believing adults. This teaching patently denies the biblical doctrine of original sin (see Psalm 51:5; Romans 5:12–21) and children's need for baptism (see Acts 2:38–41; 1 Peter 3:21).

Armageddon. (Hebrew: *har Megiddo*, or "Mount Megiddo.") A place of epic battles in the Old Testament, although there is no actual mountain at Megiddo. John makes reference to Megiddo in describing Christ's final execution of judgment against Satan, his evil forces and his followers on the Last Day (Revelation 16:16).

Beast. Revelation 13:2–18 describes two beasts: the beast of the sea (2–10; a corrupt political leader), and the beast of the earth (11–18; an evil spiritual leader; see also *Antichrist*). They work with the dragon (12:1–13:1), or Satan, and comprise an unholy trinity.

Dispensationalism. A theory distinguishing periods of time ("dispensations") in which man's obedience is tested. The most popular version of this theory has seven such periods: (1) Innocence (before the Fall); (2) Conscience (Adam to Noah); (3)

190

Government (Noah to Abraham); (4) Promise (Abraham to Moses); (5) Law (Moses to Christ); (6) Grace (the church age); and (7) Kingdom (literal millennium). Prior to John Nelson Darby, dispensationalism was relatively unknown in North America.

Eschatology. (Greek: *eschaton*, or "end.") The study of the end times, or the prophecies and writings concerning the Last Day, the second coming of Christ.

Gnosticism. An early heresy denying Christ's coming in the flesh. John refers to Gnostic teachers as "antichrists" (1 John 2:18; 4:3).

Last Days. The period of time ushered in by the arrival of Jesus Christ (see Acts 2:17; Hebrews 1:1–2). Premillennial dispensationalists see the 1948 creation of the modern state of Israel as the beginning of the Last Days.

Millennium. Literally, *millennium* is a one thousand-year period. In the Bible, the phrase "one thousand years" is used in only three verses: Psalm 90:4; 2 Peter 3:8; and Revelation 20:4. In the first two passages 1,000 years refers to the timelessness of God. In the latter verse it means the complete time of Christ's heavenly reign, beginning with His ascension through the Last Day.

Postmillennialism. The theory that Christ will return after His church rules politically on earth for a thousand years. This view was extremely popular in early American history, but few churches still hold it today.

Premillennialism. The theory that Christ will return to establish a thousand-year political rule on earth. This view was taught by John Nelson Darby in the late nineteenth century, made its way into the *Scofield Reference Bible* in the early twentieth-century, and is popularized today through the writings of Hal Lindsey, John Hagee, Tim LaHaye, Jerry Jenkins, and others.

Rapture. 1 Thessalonians 4:14–17 teaches that living believers will join resurrected believers on the Last Day with Christ. Premillennial dispensationalists teach a "secret rapture" in which Christ takes up to heaven all living Christians (and infants and young children) so that they will not suffer the tribulation. Classical premillennialist rapture teaching implied there was no hope for salvation after the rapture had taken place. The *Left Behind* book series, however, has changed that teaching by claiming that people will come to faith after Christ returns.

Tribulation. Literally, distress or suffering. Amillennialists understand tribulation passages as describing the suffering Christians currently experience. Premillennial dispensationalists anticipate a literal seven-year tribulation as part of end time events.